FINANCIAL
ADMINISTRATION
SPECIALIST UNITS

FINANCIAL ADMINISTRATION SPECIALIST UNITS

Student Handbook

Carol Carysforth
Val Warrilow

HEINEMANN

NVQ LEVEL 2

Heinemann Educational
a division of Heinemann Educational Books Ltd,
Halley Court, Jordan Hill, Oxford OX2 8EJ

OXFORD   LONDON   EDINBURGH
MADRID   ATHENS   BOLOGNA   PARIS
MELBOURNE   SYDNEY   AUCKLAND   SINGAPORE   TOKYO
IBADAN   NAIROBI   HARARE   GABORONE
PORTSMOUTH NH (USA)

First published 1991

British Library Cataloguing in Publication Data
    Carysforth, Carol
    Financial Administration: specialist units
    1. Business Practices
    I Title. II Warrilow, Valerie
    652

ISBN 0 435 450034

Designed by Green Door, Basingstoke
Illustrated by Gecko, Bicester, Oxon
Printed in England
by Clays Ltd, St Ives plc

ACKNOWLEDGEMENTS

The authors would like to personally acknowledge the co-operation, assistance and support of friends and colleagues, whose combined expertise proved invaluable in the writing of these books.

Especial thanks for specialist help and advice are due to David Williams AIDPM, Peter Gold LIB, Duncan Isherwood RIBA, John Haworth FCA, Mavis Williams Cert Ed, AFTComm, Alex Clark and, not least, Margaret Berriman for her encouragement and guidance throughout.

The authors and publishers would also like to thank the following organisations for permission to reproduce copyright material:

The Automobile Association
Banking Information Service
Barclays Bank plc – Retailer Services
Barclays Bank plc – Banking Services
British Airways plc
British Gas plc
British Rail
British Telecom plc
Air France Holidays and French Travel Service
Guardian Royal Exchange Assurance
The Controller of Her Majesty's Stationery Office
Midland Bank plc
National Westminster Bank plc – Banking Services
National Westminster Bank plc – Retailer Card Services
The Post Office
Royal Bank of Scotland plc
French Railways SNCF
Safeguard Systems GB Ltd

CONTENTS

FINANCIAL ADMINISTRATION SPECIALIST UNITS

Processing documents relating to goods and services

Section 1 – Buying and selling goods and services

There is a variety of documents used in an organisation in relation to the purchasing, sale and supply of goods and services. The specific documents with which you are involved will depend mainly on whether you are the **purchaser** or the **seller** in a particular transaction.

THE PURCHASER
Ordering goods
A small office will order goods *direct* from a local business supplier.

In a large organisation the Purchasing Department will usually order *all* the goods and services required throughout the company. This way they can buy the goods cheaper because of the discounts available on large orders.

Information can be obtained from:

- catalogues and price lists
- representatives visiting the organisation
- trade journals and magazines
- advertisements and mail shots
- trade fairs and exhibitions
- telephoning suppliers listed in Yellow Pages.

SPECIAL NOTE
Price lists are issued *separately* to catalogues so a new price list can be printed easily whenever prices change without the expense of reprinting the catalogue.

Most price lists are shown in *page order* to match the catalogue but you must be very careful to:

- check the correct catalogue number in the price list against the one shown in the catalogue, as the numbers will vary for different colours and sizes.
- Write the number *accurately* when you order (transposing the numbers will mean the wrong goods arrive and the supplier is under no obligation to take them back!)

SPECIAL NOTE

You cannot check the quality of goods from a catalogue very easily, although price may be a guide.

PURCHASING PROCEDURE AND DOCUMENTATION

1   The **buyer** looks through catalogues, telephones companies to enquire about their products or may write a **letter of enquiry**.

This asks about:

- the type of goods and range stocked by the supplier
- the price and discounts available
- delivery times and charges
- length of warranty or guarantee (if equipment)
- servicing or maintenance (if applicable).

Some organisations use special **form letters** already pre-printed with headings. They can then just complete the details and send them out to suppliers.

Other organisations store standard paragraphs on a word processor and letters of enquiry are easily written by combining the most suitable paragraphs for each particular enquiry.

SPECIAL NOTE

A buyer may advertise that he wants certain goods, or a particular service provided and ask people to submit **tenders** (offers) stating at which price they are prepared to provide the service (or supply the goods). The buyer will have a closing date for tenders to be received and, on that day, will open them and choose the best one bearing in mind price, quality, service and time of delivery.

2   The **seller** replies with a written **quotation** stating the price at which he can supply the goods and any discounts he is prepared to offer.

- **Trade discount** is given as an allowance to people in the same type of business or because the buyer is placing a large order.
- **Cash discount** is a percentage off the price given for prompt payment. The term 5% – *one month* means that the buyer can deduct 5% from the price if he pays within one month.

  Value added tax (VAT) is added to the total cost of the goods (after any discounts have been subtracted). The current rate is 15%. Full details of VAT are given in the chapter on Maintaining Financial Records.

The quotation will also show the delivery date and any delivery charges.

- **Carriage paid** means the *supplier* will pay for delivery
- **Carriage forward** means the *buyer* must pay for delivery.

SPECIAL NOTE
Instead of a quotation a supplier may issue an **estimate**. An estimate usually gives a *total* estimated price for undertaking a job or providing a particular service. It is therefore less precise than a quotation which shows an itemised list with the price of *each* item.

3   The buyer will compare quotations in terms of quality of goods, price and discounts, delivery and after-sales service (if applicable) and will send an **order** to the supplier he selects.

There will usually be *four* copies of the order:

- top copy to the supplier
- second copy to the department requesting the goods if the order is for a special item of equipment
- third copy to Accounts
- final copy kept in Purchasing.

ORDER

Coombes & Webb Ltd

15 Devonport Way
PORTSMOUTH
PR6 9KR
Tel: 0705–482937

TO: Business Supplies Ltd
14 Docklands Parade
SOUTHAMPTON

ORDER NO: 2948/90

DATE: 15 October 19

Please supply:

Quantity	Description	Catalogue Number	Unit price
250 Reams	A4 white bond paper	K/38279	£3.50 per ream
24	Red lever arch files	K/02938	£1.30 each

Delivery ....as soon as possible
Signed ....J. Taylor

SPECIAL NOTE

Other factors may also influence the buyer's decision in choosing a supplier, eg

- **reputation** is the company well-established or only new? Has the buyer dealt with them before or received good reports about them?
- **location** is the firm situated locally? (useful if goods are needed quickly or may have had to be returned or if after sales service may be required).
- **relationship** some companies have a policy of keeping to a few regular

| | suppliers to build up a good relationship with them so that they receive a personal service and priority treatment. |
| • **credit** | a supplier who offers three months' credit would usually be more attractive than one who requires payment in full within one month. |

4 The seller will despatch the goods. If he uses his own transport he will include a **delivery note** which gives details of the goods but not the price.

If he despatches the goods by another form of transport, eg by rail or by haulage company he will send the buyer an **advice note** so that the buyer knows the goods are on their way.

5 When the goods are delivered the buyer will check them against the delivery note and issue a **goods received note**. A copy of this will be sent to the Accounts Department.

6 The seller will then issue an **invoice** listing the goods and the amount owing. The buyer will check this against the goods received note and the order.

7 At the end of the month the seller will issue a **statement** showing all his transactions with the buyer that month and the total amount now due.

8 When this has been checked the buyer will pay for the goods, usually by cheque.

Routine orders
Routine orders for repeat goods from regular suppliers are commonplace in every organisation. If you are responsible for ordering goods then you should

- check that the quantity ordered allows for
  - current stock levels
  - 'lead time' (ie the gap between order and delivery)
  - availability (ie whether the goods are in short supply)
  - demand (whether it is increasing, static or decreasing
- check that the price is unchanged or still within acceptable limits

- check that discounts are still in force
- check that credit facilities are unchanged.

Any changes should be notified to your supervisor – a major change may mean a change of supplier.

Special orders

Special orders are raised for

- large items of capital equipment, eg office machinery
- services (eg supply of temporary staff from an agency, servicing and maintenance of equipment etc)
- emergency requirements.

Ordering procedures

It is important to note that these will vary from one organisation to another. All organisations are likely to follow a fairly fixed procedure for large items of expenditure, eg on capital equipment. However, small organisations may request services or emergency supplies by telephone, collect the goods if appropriate, and simply pay the invoice when it arrives.

Larger organisations will have more standard, laid-down procedures. In some firms, *nothing* must be ordered, even by telephone, without an official order number being quoted. It is therefore very important that you check the procedure in your own organisation, and keep to it!

TEST YOURSELF

1   Draft out a letter of enquiry to be sent to office equipment suppliers in your area asking about electronic typewriters. Your organisation is considering buying three new machines which must have automatic correction, automatic centring, emboldening and a memory store. The machines should be suitable for quite heavy usage.
When you have completed the letter check its contents with your tutor.

2   Use your calculator to work out which of the following would be the best buy:

a)   5 gross HB pencils @ £12.96 per gross less 10% trade discount
+ VAT

b)   5 gross HB pencils @ £1.10 dozen less 12% trade discount
+ VAT

3 Choose one item of office stationery *or* equipment or a personal item you are thinking of buying soon (eg a Walkman). Telephone at least two local suppliers and find out

- the makes or type they have in stock
- features of different makes
- (if equipment) guarantee or warranty period/service arrangements if it goes wrong
- details of prices.

Write out the details of which you would choose and why.

THE SELLER

Goods and services may be sold for cash or on **credit**.

A buyer may be given credit because:

- he has an account with the seller and is allowed to have the goods and pay for them later
- he pays by credit card in a retail establishment.

Why is credit given?

Credit is given to increase sales. It is pointless a company insisting that everyone pays cash with their order if all their competitors allow their customers credit. People also expect to pay for many items some time after they buy them and when one business sells to another the giving of some credit is the usual practice.

In business, a customer who is allowed to buy on credit has his or her own account with the supplier. This means there will be an account under his or her name in the organisation's Sales Ledger and every time he or she buys goods, an entry will be made in that account. Similarly when the customer pays for goods this will also be recorded in the ledger. At the end of every month the details of his or her account are listed to produce a **statement** which is sent to that person so that the state of the account with that organisation at the end of that month is known – the amount owed by the customer bearing in mind all purchases and any payments made for these.

The organisation will now expect the customer to settle his or her account by paying the balance shown on the statement, usually by cheque.

Credit control

The amount of credit given to individual customers and the total amount of outstanding debts owed to a company *must* be controlled. Otherwise the number of **bad debts** (debts which are never paid) would be tremendous and the company would go out of business.

Not all customers are given the same amount of credit. (Similarly, not all credit card holders are allowed the same amount of credit with banks and stores). The total amount each customer is allowed – and whether that customer is allowed any at all – will depend on their **credit rating**. This is based on the customer's financial position and past history and on whether they are good or bad payers.

The credit rating for customers will usually be set by a Credit Controller in a company and must *never* be exceeded. Therefore a check must be kept continuously that the total amount owed by each customer does not exceed the total credit they are allowed. The Credit Controller will decide on the rating from a number of possible sources.

- Credit agency ratings – an organisation can subscribe to a company such as Dun & Bradstreet which issues ratings on companies based on their published accounts.
- Trade associations who have their own credit reference departments and provide information regarding 'blacklisted' companies. Examples of trade associations are the Motor Traders' association and the Building Trades' association.
- Bankers' references.
- Trade references – the potential customer is asked to provide

two or three references from other people in business who have dealt with him or her over some time.

- Sales representatives can often supply useful information.

The higher the rating the customer is eventually given, the greater the credit he or she is allowed.

Checking credit

Sales staff need to be able to liaise quickly with accounts staff to check the state of customer accounts.

- The sales staff can telephone the ledger clerk giving the name of the customer and the amount. The ledger clerk checks the state of the account and either sanctions or refuses the sale. (In some very large companies the sales ledger is divided up according to the letters of the alphabet with one ledger clerk dealing with each letter or group of letters).
- A separate card index is kept in the sales department and the credit limit is shown by a coloured signal. Special tags are attached for customers both nearing their limit and over their limit.
- The accounts department issues a regularly updated list (preferably daily) of customers who must not be given any further credit. In some organisations this is known as a **stop list**.
  This information is taken from the Aged Debtors Account.

Discuss with your tutor:

- how the account can quickly be checked to make sure it balances accurately
- the methods the company will use to chase up money due to them.

BALANCE AT 1st March

BALANCE OWING	ACCOUNT	b/F	LAST IN MONTH	ONE MONTH	TWO MONTHS	THREE MONTHS	FOUR MONTHS
6274 40	Balance	b/o	4972 20	643 80	387 30	205 50	65 60
62 20	J Seed Ltd	1	41 00	21 20			
15 00	T Shepherd	2	15 00				
38 50	Smedley and Sons Ltd	3		16 50	22 00		
224 40	Tatton and West Ltd	4	84 20	73 80	66 40		
46 60	B Tidswell	5			19 60	27 00	
607 32	Topham Plant Hire	6	122 18	201 60		120 14	163 40
106 30	Unity Transport	7				16 00	90 30
203 90	Walker and Maine Ltd	8	113 20	80 50		10 20	
60 24	P Whiteside and Co	9	40 16	20 08			
15 00	J York and Co	10					15 00
7653 86		11	5387 94	1057 48	495 30	378 84	334 30
		12					

Technology update

Computerised accounts and 'smart' cards have revolutionised credit control:

- All customer accounts are kept on computer and can be accessed from a variety of terminals. Alternatively the order details can be keyed in and checked automatically against the status of the account.
- The account status can be transmitted to electronic tills. When the customer account number is keyed in, the account is checked automatically before the till will process the sale.
- Credit cards are put through a 'reader' attached to the tills and the account status is automatically checked.
- 'Smart' cards record information on to the card itself. Each customer has his or her own card and this is put into a special part of the till. The total amount for the sale is deducted

automatically from the total credit limit and the balance 'held' on the card, (eg a Phonecard).

Discounts and time allowed for payment

Customers are often allowed different amounts of discount and different lengths of time in which to pay. This usually depends on the volume of business done between the two companies. Traders who buy in large quantities will obviously be given better trade discounts. Those who are established, regular customers may be given longer to settle their accounts or a cash discount incentive to encourage prompt payment. This means the company will receive their money quicker and keep the total amount of money owing to them as low as possible.

TEST YOURSELF

1   Your company offers trade discounts of 5% on orders from £50 to £100, 10% on orders between £100 and £800 and 15% on orders of £800 and over. You have received the following orders. Work out the discount on each.
   - Item 4028A, 4 @ £63.50 + Item 2839, 6 @ £17.83 + Item 4931, 8 @ £53.72 + Item 3746, 17 @ £23.30.
   - Item 2718, 6 @ £9.68 + Item 2736, 2 @ £12.85.

2   A company receives an invoice totalling £1873.45, terms 2½%/10 days. What will be the saving if it pays promptly?

SALES PROCEDURE AND DOCUMENTATION

TEST YOURSELF

As the seller of the goods you are now responsible for *sending* the quotation in response to an enquiry. From the work you did earlier under Purchasing Procedure and Documentation, can you list the information which must be included on a quotation?

Types of enquiry

Enquiries may be received by letter or by telephone. If you cannot help the caller quickly then arrange to ring them back when you have looked up the information you require.

In many cases callers may want advice or help on which item would be the most suitable for their purpose, in addition to details of price.

For large items it is usual to follow up with a written quotation. For some goods it may be necessary for a representative to call to ascertain the potential buyer's exact needs and the quotation will be prepared following his or her visit.

Information on goods available, price, discounts, delivery and so on may be available from:

- catalogues and price lists
- enquiry information packs assembled by the company containing stock lists, prices and delivery information etc.
- a computer database. All the information is stored on computer and enquiries can be quickly dealt with by the operator accessing the stock lists on his or her own terminal.

Types of quotation

A written quotation may be prepared on a standard form and be sent with a short letter attached to make the response more personal or alternatively a form letter may be completed.

eg

SUPRA OFFICE SUPPLIES LTD

24 Rochester Way
CANTERBURY

Tel: 0227–637251

Mr K Harrison   **QUOTATION**
Buyer
Barnes & Goodman Ltd
Unit 4
Mile End Industrial Complex
ASHFORD
Kent   TN23 8AL

15 February 19__

To   Supply and delivery of

One Suprex FE 2839 plain paper copier	£1855.00
Automatic document feeder	£980.00
10 bin sorter	£800.00
	£3635.00

All prices subject to VAT @ 15%

Trade Discount 5%

Terms 2½/10 days

Delivery within 7 days of receipt of order

Signed   ....

Standard letters

A quotation such as the one above may be accompanied by a short standard letter. This would:

- thank the potential buyer for his/her enquiry
- mention the enclosed quotation and say that if there are any queries the enquirer should contact the writer
- end by saying that the writer hopes to receive their order.

If there are any special factors to be taken into consideration these would also be included.

TEST YOURSELF

Write a short standard letter following the information given above to accompany the quotation. The sender will be Miss J Evans, Sales Manager.

Invoices

When an order has been received and the goods have been delivered, an **invoice** is prepared and sent to the buyer.

All invoices have the letters **E&OE** at the bottom. This stands for *errors and omissions excepted*. It means that if there are any mistakes or items missed off, the supplier has the right to send a supplementary invoice to charge the extra amount still owing.

The total amount shown on an invoice will vary, depending on whether there is cash discount allowable or not.

CHECK IT YOURSELF

Compare the two invoices on page 14. What is the difference between them?

The difference is in the terms offered, and therefore the amount of VAT.

- VAT is levied on both the goods and any delivery charge.
- If the goods are supplied with cash discount available it is assumed that the buyer will want to take advantage of this. In the above example, if the buyer paid within 10 days he would pay £333 – £16.65 (5%) = £316.35 for the goods. The VAT is calculated on *this* figure – 15% of £316.35 = £47.45.
- The VAT for the delivery charge must then be added to the VAT for the goods to calculate the total amount of VAT.

Invoice 1

T ROSS LTD
Craiglands Industrial Estate
EXETER 5EX 9PF

Vat Reg No
483/28372/75

Tel: 0392-384726
Fax: 0392-398273

INVOICE

TO: J Watts & Co Ltd
15 Sandown Road
PLYMOUTH
PL2 8DK

DELIVER TO:
14 Trafalgar Street
PLYMOUTH
PL1 9FP

Your Order No	Invoice Date Tax point	Invoice no	Despatch date
K/3847	2 March 199-	PS/29837	2 March 199-

Quantity	Description	Cat No	Unit price	Total price	VAT rate	VAT amount
20	'Royal' Personal Stereo Sets	YL 29	£18.50	370.00		
	Less 10% Trade Discount			37.00		
				333.00	15%	47.45*

Delivery charges	5.00	15%	0.75
Sub-total	338.00		
VAT	48.20		
Total amount due	386.20		

Terms: 5%/10 days

E & O E

* Based on cash discounted price

Invoice 2

T ROSS LTD
Craiglands Industrial Estate
EXETER 5EX 9PF

Vat Reg No
483/28372/75

Tel: 0392-384726
Fax: 0392-398273

INVOICE

TO: J Watts & Co Ltd
15 Sandown Road
PLYMOUTH
PL2 8DK

DELIVER TO:
14 Trafalgar Street
PLYMOUTH
PL1 9FP

Your Order No	Invoice Date Tax point	Invoice no	Despatch date
K/3847	2 March 199-	PS/29837	2 March 199-

Quantity	Description	Cat No	Unit price	Total price	VAT rate	VAT amount
20	'Royal' Personal Stereo Sets	YL 29	£18.50	370.00		
	Less 10% Trade Discount			37.00		
				333.00	15%	49.95

Delivery charges	5.00	15%	0.75
Sub-total	338.00		
VAT	50.70		
Total amount due	388.70		

Terms: Net monthly

E & O E

SPECIAL NOTE

- Remember! If this invoice is settled within 10 days the amount owing is £316.35 (the discounted price) + £48.20 VAT = £364.55 *not* £386.20.
- If the invoice is settled *after* ten days the full amount for the goods is due but the VAT figure *does not change*. The buyer therefore pays the total amount shown on the invoice of £386.20.

TEST YOURSELF

Goods are sold for £625 less 10% trade discount. 7½% cash discount is offered if the invoice is settled within 10 days. Delivery is £8 extra.

1 What is the total VAT which will be shown on the invoice?
2 What is the total amount due if the company pays within ten days?
3 How much is payable after this time?

Invoice sets and distribution

Invoices are often prepared on special **invoice sets** made of NCR (no carbon required) paper. Each set may consist of as many as six or seven documents:

1 *Top copy* = **invoice**. Sent to customer *after* the goods have been delivered.
2 *Second copy* = **copy invoice**. Sent to accounts department for entries to be made in customer sales ledger and sales day book.
3 *Third copy* = **advice note**. Sent to customer to inform him the goods are on their way. Does not show price or VAT.
4 *Fourth copy* = **despatch note**. Sent to despatch department for goods to be packed and sent. Stock levels are also adjusted from this copy and a note made of any items out of stock or to follow. Again does not show prices or VAT.
5 *Fifth copy* = **delivery note**. Sent to customer with the goods. Again

adjusted for out of stock items. There may be two copies of the delivery note – the customer signs both to acknowledge receipt. The customer keeps one and the driver brings the other back to the organisation as proof of delivery. Again this document contains no prices or VAT.

6 *Sixth copy* = **copy invoice**. Retained by sales department for their records.

The fact that no prices or VAT are shown on certain copies presents no problem. Invoice packs are designed so that this information will not transfer onto the advice, despatch and delivery note.

TEST YOURSELF

1 Make out an invoice to J Watts for 50 sets of earphones, catalogue number PT 434 @ £3.50 each plus VAT less 5% trade discount. Their order number was M/3827 and our invoice is 302839. Delivery will be in 3 days' time to Trafalgar Street and the charge is £3. Terms are net monthly.

2 Now make out a second invoice for the same goods. This time the terms are 2½%/7 days.

Pro forma invoices

These are special invoices issued when

- Goods must be paid for *before* delivery. In this case the pro forma is issued because the supplier does not know the buyer – and therefore wants payment in advance. The pro forma is therefore an 'offer to buy' – unless this offer is taken up, the goods will not be despatched.

- Goods are sent on sale or return. In this case the buyer will have a limited time to decide whether he is keeping all, some or none of the goods – and a limited time in which to pay. If he is keeping them all he merely pays the pro forma in full. If he is returning some of them then he sends back both the unwanted goods *and* the pro forma invoice and a final invoice is issued based on the number retained.

A pro forma invoice *cannot* be used for VAT purposes. It is therefore always clearly marked **'This is not a Tax Invoice'**. If the customer pays for the goods then a proper tax invoice must then be issued and sent to him.

SPECIAL NOTE

An alternative method of making a new buyer pay for the goods 'up front' is to send the goods COD. This means the buyer must pay **Cash On Delivery**. If the total amount to be collected is £50 or under, then the postman will collect the money at the door on delivery. If the amount is between £50 and £350 then the customer is sent a card, asking him/her to collect the goods and pay for them at the sorting office. COD is not available on goods over £350 in value.

An invoice will usually be included with the goods, for the buyer's records, but will be clearly marked 'Cash On Delivery'.

Supplementary invoices (debit notes)

If a mistake is made on an invoice and too *little* is charged then the supplier will issue a **supplementary invoice** for the additional amount. This may happen if:

- the goods were undercharged
- too many or better goods were sent and kept
- an item was omitted from the invoice.

A supplementary invoice used to be called a **debit note** but this term has gone out of use in most offices. A supplementary invoice is made out in exactly the same way as an ordinary one.

Credit notes

A **credit note** is sent if the supplier has charged too *much* on the invoice. This may happen if:

- the goods were overcharged
- some goods are returned to the supplier
- fewer were delivered than stated on the invoice.

At one time all credit notes were printed in red, though this is not usually the case today.

CHECK IT YOURSELF

- Why do you think most organisations today print credit notes in black?
- How many reasons can you think of why goods may be returned to the supplier?

Examine the credit note below. Note that the trade discount and the cash discount on the credit note must be *identical* to that shown on the original invoice.

T ROSS LTD

Craiglands Industrial Estate
EXETER 5EX 9PF

Tel: 0392-384726
Fax: 0392-398273

Vat Reg No
483/28372/75

CREDIT NOTE

TO: J Watts & Co Ltd
15 Sandown Road
PLYMOUTH
PL2 8DK

Credit Note No	Invoice No	Date
CR 2837	PS/29837	14 March 19_

Quantity	Description	Cat No	Unit price	Total price	VAT rate	VAT amount
2	'Royal' Personal Stereo Sets (Returned)	YL 29	£18.50	£37.00		
	Less 10% Trade Discount			3.70		
				£33.30	15%	£4.75*

	Delivery Charges		
	Sub-total	£33.30	
	VAT	4.75	
Terms: 5%/10 days	Total amount due	38.05	

E & O E

* Cash discounted price

- How much would the VAT amount have been if there had been no cash discount?
- Carriage may sometimes be shown on a credit note. This means the supplier is crediting (refunding) carriage expenses incurred by the buyer. Discuss with your tutor occasions when suppliers would be prepared to refund carriage paid returning goods, and occasions when they wouldn't.

TEST YOURSELF

Assume that our company (T Ross Ltd) only delivered 45 sets of earphones to J Watts and not the 50 sets you invoiced previously. Make out a credit note for the 5 sets you overcharged. Use the same information as before. The credit note number is CR 2842.

- The first time assume there is no cash discount (terms: net monthly).
- The second time assume the terms on the original invoice were 2½%/7 days.

Statements

At the end of each month the supplier sends a **statement** to each of his customers. This is a statement of the customer's account, taken from the Sales Ledger, at a certain date.

STATEMENT		Number __428637__		
		Date ___30 June 199–__		
Daniel & Sons 22 Ainsley Park Wolverhampton WV4 8LR		VAT Registration Number 293/273648/73		
TO: __Markham & Ellis Ltd__ __14 Priory Walk__ __SHREWSBURY SW2 1JP__		Account No.___6342___		

Date	Particulars	Debit	Credit	Balance
1 June	Balance			£489.00
3 June	Cheque		£132.00	£621.00
9 June	Cheque		£300.00	£321.00
15 June	Invoice S 58279	£231.42		£552.42
19 June	Credit Note CR 542		£36.80	£515.62
24 June	Invoice S 62892	£929.70		£1145.32
28 June	Cheque	£42.18		£1487.50
30 June	Invoice S 70982	£232.90		£1720.40

Below is shown the statement which would be sent to J Watts for the transactions which took place during March, including the sale and credit of the stereo sets. The figures are taken from the invoice and credit note showing cash discount.

T ROSS LTD

Craiglands Industrial Estate
EXETER 5EX 9PF

Tel: 0392–384726
Fax: 0392–398272

Vat Reg No
483/28372/75

STATEMENT

TO: J Watts & Co Ltd
15 Sandowne Road
PLYMOUTH
PL2 8DJ

Date: 31 March 19__

Account No: /45/298

Date	Description	Debit	Credit	Balance
1 March	Balance			£125.00
2 March	Invoice PF/25837	£470.71		595.71
7 March	Cheque		£125.00	470.71
14 March	Credit Note CR 2837		38.50	432.21

Total now due: £432.21

! SPECIAL NOTE

- The **debit** column shows amounts owing to the supplier.
- The **credit** column shows deductions from this, eg payments and credit notes.
- The **balance** column is completed after each transaction.

TEST YOURSELF

1   Why did J Watts pay a cheque for £125 on 7 March?
2   Test your proof-reading skills! Although this statement has been compiled
    from information on the invoice and credit note there are five errors. Can you
    find and correct them?

SPECIAL NOTE

Throughout this section you should have noticed that the buying and selling of
goods, and the documentation required, calls for a considerable amount of
liaison between departments.

- Liaison between the Purchasing Department and the Accounts Department
  regarding the price of goods ordered, time allowed for payment, discounts,
  and special requirements, etc. Notifying the Accounts Department when
  goods have been received, if there are any discrepancies etc.
- Liaison between the Sales Department and the Accounts Department
  regarding the price of goods sold, credit terms given, discounts, etc.
  Notifying the Accounts Department when goods have been delivered, if
  there are any returns or other adjustments to take into account.
- Liaison between Sales Department and the Accounts Department regarding
  credit rating of different customers.

Remember – no one department can ever work in isolation if the organisation is
to function effectively.

SECTION REVIEW

Having completed this section, you should now be able to:

1   Identify the documents concerned with the buying and
    selling of goods.

2   Differentiate between cash and trade discount.

3   State the criteria involved in selecting a supplier.

4   Compose a letter of enquiry.

5   Differentiate between a tender, an estimate and a quotation.

6   Explain how ordering procedures may vary between small
    and large organisations.

7   Issue quotations.

8 Issue VAT invoices which include trade and/or cash discount and transport charges.

9 Explain the terms pro forma invoice and COD.

10 Issue credit notes.

11 Issue statements.

12 Explain the importance of credit control and the methods by which this is achieved.

13 Explain the importance of liaison between purchasing, sales and accounts departments.

REVIEW QUIZ

True or false?

1 VAT is calculated on an invoice after trade discount has been deducted.

2 The credit column of a statement shows payments made against the account.

3 The advice note is used by stock control to adjust stock levels for goods going out.

4 Carriage is never shown on a credit note.

5 A supplementary invoice is issued if the customer has been undercharged on the original invoice

Complete the blanks ...

6 The letters E&OE stand for ....

7 The balance column on a statement is completed after
....

8 A .... may be sent in response to enquiries regarding goods and prices.

Work it out

9 Make out an invoice to M Hines & Co, Briarhill Industrial Estate, Mere Park, Stafford, ST5 9EM for

20 Country Maid toasters @ £16 each plus VAT
12 Country Maid jug kettles @ £18.50 each plus VAT

Their order number was 3829/90 and your invoice no is KY/39283.

Date it today. Your organisation allows 10% trade discount and terms are 2½%/10 days.

10 After a week Hines returns two toasters as they are faulty. Make out a credit note.

11 At the beginning of the month Hines' account showed a balance of £217.50. They have sent two cheques during the month – one for £75 on the 4th and one for £110 and the 21st.

Make out a statement at the end of the month showing these transactions and the amount in the invoice and credit note you have calculated.

12 A quotation you are preparing shows the goods will cost £4012.20 + VAT. Your company offers a trade discount of 7½% and terms are 5%/7 days. Work out how much the goods will cost:

a if the organisation takes a month to pay the account

b if the organisation pays within 7 days.

Section 2 – Reconciling invoices and processing expense claims for payment

Look back to the statement at the end of the previous section. How many errors did you find? What would have been the result for your organisation if you had paid it without checking it?

All accounts documents must be carefully checked and only paid when it has been established that they are correct.

RECONCILING INVOICES FOR PAYMENT

Goods invoices

To reconcile goods invoices for payment, you first need to assemble the other documents relating to the goods, ie the Quotation and/or Order, and the Goods Received Note and/or Delivery Note.

In most organisations it is usual for copies of all relevant documents, and the Delivery Note itself, to be sent to the Accounts Department.

Stage 1 – Check the invoice against the quotation/copy order

- is the quantity correct?
- do the descriptions match?
- are all the prices as quoted?
- is the discount correct?
- do the terms of payment match?
- were you/are you liable for transport charges?

Stage 2 – Check the invoice against the GRN or Delivery Note

- were all the goods delivered?
- were they all in good condition on arrival?

Stage 3 – Check the figures

- are all the calculations accurate?
- is the date correct?

Stage 4 – If this is a VAT invoice

- is the supplier registered for VAT?
- is the tax point correct? (see page 26)

Stage 5 – Check the file

- is this a duplicate invoice sent by mistake?

Stage 6 – Approve invoice for payment.

SPECIAL NOTE

In many large organisations the Stores Section will send up a list of deliveries and the checks will be made from this – not the delivery notes themselves, which are retained by Stores. Only if there is a discrepancy will a delivery note itself be referred to.

Service invoices

Invoices for services may be more difficult to check as the accounts staff cannot be expected to know whether the service provided was carried out at the right time, and undertaken properly. The procedure in many companies is for specified managers to be responsible for authorising the payments of certain services.

Again, however, calculations and the risk of duplication must still be checked before the invoice is approved for payment.

Sales and geographical references

All organisations should have properly laid down procedures for checking invoices – it should not be the job of the Accounts Clerk to have to hunt around the company to find out who ordered what, and if/when it was delivered!

To solve this problem, large organisations often adopt a reference system, so that the office or person responsible for the order is clearly identifiable by looking at the reference. Therefore a large Head Office could determine which of its branch offices had ordered the goods or service, and the executive responsible.

VAT invoices

VAT invoices need special care as your organisation can *reclaim* the VAT paid when it completes its VAT Return at the end of the quarter. (VAT is dealt with in full in the chapter on Maintaining Financial Records).

A feature of VAT invoices is the **tax point**, usually shown separately to the date of the invoice. Usually you will find that this corresponds to the date of the invoice, and it indicates the date that the title to (right to own) the goods was transferred from the seller to the buyer. However, there are certain exceptions when the dates may not match, eg:

- if cash is paid as the goods are collected (in this case no invoice will be issued). In this case the tax point is the date when payment is made.

- if the goods are issued on sale or return. In this case a pro forma invoice may have been issued (see last section) *not* a Tax invoice. The tax point is the date at the end of the sale or return period. If, however, the customer accepts the goods before the end of this period then this date is the tax point.

- if an item is built on site (eg an extension to a building) then the tax point is the date the item is made available for the customer to use.

The tax point indicates the period in which VAT was charged. It is not, therefore, legal to hand goods over to a person and defer invoicing them so that the VAT is due at a later date (see *VAT Guidelines* for further details).

PROCESSING INVOICES FOR PAYMENT

- Ideally a variety of people should be involved in checking the

invoice. It should *not* just be the responsibility of one person, especially if it is for a very large amount of money.
- Usually the document is stamped with a rubber stamp showing the stages it must pass through. As each person carries out their function they initial the appropriate box.

ACCOUNT VERIFICATION		
Item	**Status**	**Verified By**
Goods received Invoice details as Quote/Order Invoice correct		
Payment approved . . . . (Signed)		

SPECIAL NOTE

- In very large companies it may be uneconomic to employ someone to check every invoice, especially those for very small amounts. In this case invoices over a certain figure, eg £100 would be checked and smaller totals would be *batch* checked, ie certain invoices would be checked at random.

CHECK IT YOURSELF

- Why do you think most organisations prefer several people to check accounts documents *as well* as the person making the payments?
- Check the invoice extract shown on page 28. Assuming the terms are correct and the goods were delivered, as ordered, in good condition, would you be prepared to authorise it for payment?
- If not, list all the errors you can find and then calculate the correct amounts.

INVOICE EXTRACT

Quantity	Description	Cat No	Unit price	Total price	VAT rate	VAT amount
22	Regency swivel chairs	283	£96.50	£2132.00		
2	Regency Executive chairs	286	£138.20	£276.40		
8	Visitors' chairs	288	£52.00	£418.00		
2	Reception Stools	296	58.00	£58.00		
	Less 10% Trade Discount			£2784.00		
				278.40		
				£3062.80	15%	£459.42
	Delivery charges			18.00	15%	£2.50
	Sub-total			£3080.80		
	VAT			461.29		
	Total amount due			£3542.72		

Terms: net monthly

E & O E

Problem solving

If you find a mistake or discrepancy in any invoice you must know how to deal with it. The procedure may differ depending on whether you work for a large organisation, when it would be referred to the supervisor, or in a small one – when you may have to sort it out yourself.

If you are on your own, first calculate the amount the invoice should be and then double check you are still right!

- If the discrepancy is small and the organisation is one you deal with regularly then you could probably ring them up to point out the error. They may say they will issue a replacement invoice but they are more likely to issue a supplementary invoice or a credit note for the difference.

- If the discrepancy is large or if you do not know anyone personally at the organisation it is better to write to them. This means the correspondence will be on file and can be referred to if there is any dispute.

- If there are regular discrepancies from one particular organisation you may want to write a more formal letter of complaint and this would be signed by your manager.

SPECIAL NOTE

A *reputable* company points out errors whether they are being overcharged or undercharged! Most companies would rather keep their reputation than save a few pounds by keeping quiet about a mistake which will probably be discovered by the supplier at a later date!

Paying the account

When the invoice has been passed for payment then the Accounts Department will pay the supplier, usually by cheque. However, in many cases the company waits until a Statement has been received from the supplier, listing all the invoices, credit notes and payments made that month, and the balance owing to date. They are less likely to wait, however, if they can take advantage of cash discount terms by paying more promptly.

EXPENSE CLAIMS

Expense claims are completed by many employees, either on a regular or occasional basis. Employees who often incur expenses on behalf of their organisation, eg representatives, may have an expense account, as will executives of the company. However, other employees without an expense account may be in the position of claiming back money if, for instance, they visit another company and incur travel expenses.

Most organisations set a limit to their expense accounts – no executive or representative is normally allowed to exceed the limit unless there is a very good reason. Any employee claiming back money should always keep, and attach, a receipt for all items to his or her expense claim.

SPECIAL NOTE

Some organisations issue their executives with credit cards – and the accounts from the credit card companies must also be checked against the expense claims and expense account limit.

Expense codes

Expenses are usually claimed for the following types of item:

- travel fares or mileage if the employee's own car is used
- company car expenses, eg petrol, car parking, repair bills
- meals whilst away on company business (often called 'subsistence')
- business entertaining
- hotel expenses.

Each type of expense will have an expense code – and a code column is included on expense forms which is usually completed by the clerk who checks the claim. The code enables the organisation to analyse expenses to see:

- how much is being spent on each category of expense
- whether the total expenditure on each category exceeds budget limits
- the total amount of the expenses which can be allowed against tax.

Expenses and tax

If an employee can be seen, in any way, to benefit from an expense payment made by his firm then he may have to pay tax on this additional benefit. For instance, if a company director took his wife with him on a trip, and was given £500 to pay for the trip, the taxman would usually consider that participation by the wife was a 'bonus' and the amount claimed for her expenses is taxable.

Virtually all organisations negotiate with their Tax Office which expenses are essential for their employees. A firm which exports may entertain very many foreign customers and would therefore be able to negotiate higher business entertainment expenses for its executives than a firm which only dealt with UK firms. Negotiated expenses are known as a **dispensation** – and no tax is payable on expenses to which the dispensation applies.

Each employer has to give the Inland Revenue details of all fringe benefits and expense allowances paid to employees who earn (currently) more than £8 500 a year using form **P11D**. A copy is also given to the employee. This form also shows which expense payments will be **taxable**, ie:

- if a representative is paid a fixed daily expense allowance, then any amount above the dispensation amount will be taxable
- if a company pays all the home telephone bills of an employee then this amount is usually taxable
- if a company pays for health insurance, ie in a BUPA scheme then this amount is also taxable
- business entertaining is a 'grey' area – a proportion may be taxable if it is seen as a benefit to the employee
- if an amount is paid for petrol (rather than just for mileage) it will be assumed that some of the petrol has been used for private motoring (or for getting from home to work) and therefore a proportion will be taxable.

Non-taxable expense payments include *all* amounts for which dispensation has been agreed, mileage payments and other payments for tax 'allowable' expenses.

Tax allowable expenses

If an expense is incurred 'wholly, exclusively and necessarily' in the performance of the duties of employment then the expense is allowable against tax. Not only is no tax paid on this, but tax relief is given by the Inland Revenue to the person or the organisation – depending on who has sustained the expense. Therefore if the company reimburses the employee then the company claims the tax relief. If the employee pays the expense himself then he or she can claim back for the expense on his or her Tax Return.

Allowable expenses include:

- car repairs and expenses
- hotel expenses
- protective clothing and uniforms
- training fees for a course to improve work-related skills
- essential reference books and *business* stationery
- travel on business trips
- subscriptions to professional bodies (work-related).

Non-allowable expenses include:

- expenditure on ordinary clothes
- examination or resit fees
- travel between home and business
- fines for breaking the law, eg parking fines
- interest on credit cards
- ordinary meals (eg at or near workplace).

SPECIAL NOTE

The area of tax, expenses and allowances is extremely complicated and contains many 'grey' areas. For this reason, any queries you have *must* be referred to your supervisor or the company's accountant for clarification.

Company allowable expenses

The expenses that an organisation will allow differ considerably from one organisation to another. Some are very progressive, others less so. Some companies have negotiated a number of dispensations with the Inland Revenue, others have not – much will depend on the size of the company, the business they are in, whether they export, etc.

All tax allowable expenses will usually be acceptable as the company can reimburse the employee and then claim tax relief itself. Generally, most non-allowable expenses are not acceptable – although there may be exceptions such as payments for meals or examination fees where the company is willing to bear the expense even though tax relief cannot be claimed.

It is important that you check *which* expenses are allowable by any organisation for which you work:

- if you are checking expense claims
- if you are submitting expense claims.

Advances

Executives or representatives who are going on a business trip, and are not issued with a credit card, may be given an advance payment rather than be expected to pay out a large amount from their own pocket. A record of the advance is made and this, obviously, is deducted from the expense claim before repayment is made. If the advance is not used in full then the difference must be repaid to the company. If the executive was allowed to retain the difference then this amount would be taxable.

CHECK IT YOURSELF

You work for a large organisation where the MD and the executives keep a high profile in the community. When you process their expense claims you notice several items you haven't met before.

Which do you think will be taxable and which non-taxable? Discuss your answers with your tutor.

1 Expenses incurred for home entertaining, drinks accounts etc.
2 Paris hotel bill incurred whilst visiting French customer.
3 Wardrobe allowance for female MD.
4 Air travel expenses to visit a client in New York.
5 Membership of the local golf club for all executives.
6 Membership fees to the Institute of Directors.

Processing expense claims for payment

On receipt, expense claims should be checked to ensure:

- all receipts are attached
- all relevant columns are completed
- all calculations are correct
- all expenses claimed are allowed by the firm
- any advance has been recorded and deducted from the total
- all mileage claims are accurate. (Most offices keep their own mileage charts for checking.)

The accounts clerk then:

- enters the expense codes for each item
- signs the form
- passes it for payment *or* to the supervisor for authorisation for payment.

Some organisations add the amount to be repaid to the person's next wage or salary. Others repay expenses separately, eg once a week. In this case the amount received must be signed for by the recipient who usually has to collect it personally.

Dealing with discrepancies

- Mistakes in calculations, wrong claims and missing receipts are usually dealt with by referring the problem back to the person who completed the form. If the mistake is only minor the form may be altered and initialled by the clerk. Rather than make several alterations on a form, however, it is usual to make out another, and destroy the first.
- Staff who regularly complete the forms wrongly should be referred to the staff handbook or leaflet showing them how this should be done correctly.
- Claims for excessive amounts should be referred to your supervisor.

CHECK IT YOURSELF

- If you are working then get a copy of your company's expense claim form. If you are full-time student then your tutor should be able to show you a copy of a College form.

- Work through with your tutor how this should be completed and note the columns and the layout of the forms.
- If possible, compare several different forms – note where columns and headings are the same and where they differ.
- Check the procedure for reimbursing expenses which operates in your organisation.

VAT and expenses

On virtually all expense claim forms you will see a separate column for VAT. This is because VAT is levied on all VAT-chargeable goods and services sold by companies registered for VAT. If your company is also registered for VAT then a separate record must always be kept of how much is paid out on VAT so that it can be reclaimed on the VAT Return.

Therefore, when someone submits an expense claim the amount paid is split into the net amount and the VAT paid to give the total amount paid.

The VAT column is easy to complete when the VAT amount is listed separately on a receipt – known as **plus** VAT. However, in other cases the amount paid is VAT **inclusive**, ie not listed separately. For instance, if you buy food in McDonalds or petrol in a garage the amount you are charged is inclusive of VAT – you are not told how much the VAT is.

In these cases it may be the job of the accounts clerk to calculate the VAT inclusive amount.

To work out VAT inclusive amounts

A representative spends £88 on petrol in a week. The VAT rate is 15%.

$$\text{VAT} = \frac{15}{115} \quad \frac{\text{(rate of VAT)}}{\text{(VAT rate + 100)}}$$

If you have a calculator then enter 88 × 15 ÷ 115. (Don't forget to round your answer to two decimal places.)

You should have made the answer £11.48.

To find the answer *exclusive* of VAT you can either

a) subtract the amount of VAT from the total paid (£88 − £11.48 = £76.52), *or*

b) calculate it as follows:

$$\text{Exclusive price} = \frac{100}{115} \quad \frac{(100)}{(\text{VAT rate} + 100)}$$

On a calculator enter 88 × 100 ÷ 115. You should get £76.52.

SPECIAL NOTE

The second option (b) is the best method because it gives you a double check. The amount of the exclusive price + the VAT must equal the total amount spent.

VAT rate changes

The formulae can be applied for any rate of VAT.

$$\text{Therefore VAT rate 10\%} \quad \text{VAT} = \frac{10}{110} \quad \text{VAT exclusive} = \frac{100}{110}$$

TEST YOURSELF

If the government changed the VAT rate to:

- 5%
- 20%

what formulae would you use?

Cancelling down

Rather than using large figures all the time, it is better to cancel down fractions if possible.

For the current rate of VAT (15%), the VAT formulae cancel down as follows:

$$\text{VAT} = \frac{15}{115} = \frac{3}{23} \quad \text{VAT exclusive} = \frac{100}{115} = \frac{20}{23}$$

Test it – work out the calculations for petrol at £88 again – this time using the cancelled down formulae. You should get the same answers!

Work out the cancelled down formulae if VAT is

- 10%
- 5%
- 20%

Confidentiality

Whatever documents you process in an accounts section you must be aware that your work will be of a confidential nature and *not* discuss

- which organisations are bad payers and how much they owe
- which members of staff can't add up or work out their expenses properly
- the actions (and/or mistakes) of their colleagues.

Treat others as you would like to be treated yourself – the next mistake might be your own!

SECTION REVIEW

Having completed this section, you should now be able to:

1 Identify and rectify discrepancies and errors in invoices.

2 Explain the term **tax point**.

3 Describe the procedures for checking goods and service invoices.

4 Explain how checked invoices are processed for payment.

5 Explain how sales and geographical references can assist invoice processing.

6 Identify and rectify discrepancies and errors on expense claims.

7 Differentiate between taxable and non-taxable expenses.

8 Differentiate between those expenses the company will allow and those for which no claim can be made.

9 Explain when an advance may be paid to an employee.

10 Calculate VAT inclusive amounts.

11 Explain how expense claims are processed for payments.

12 Explain the relevance of confidentiality to accounts work.

REVIEW QUIZ

True or false?

1 The term tax point is seen on *all* invoices.

2 VAT is always shown separately on receipts.

3 Expense codes are used to categorise expenditure.

4 The date of an invoice is usually the same as the tax point date.

5 Only VAT registered suppliers can charge VAT on items they sell.

Complete the blanks . . .

6 The letters GRN stand for ....

7 The current rate of VAT is ....

8 The form sent to the Tax Office by the company (with a copy to the employee) detailing expenses paid is the ....

Work it out

9 Opposite is shown the expense claim form of Ian Bretherton, a new employee who started with your company last month.

    a Check his expense claim carefully. List any errors you can find and then calculate the correct amounts. (Assume that his claim that he hasn't received any advances is correct).

    b Calculate the amounts, excluding VAT, and the VAT columns for all the petrol entries, at the current VAT rate. Note that the taxi fare is *not* liable for VAT.

    c Work out the new totals and the final amount due.

d What documents should Mr Bretherton have attached as evidence of his claims?

BRYANTS & COLE LTD

EXPENSE CLAIM FORM

NAME IAN BRETHERTON		EMPLOYEE NO 4398		WEEK ENDING 5/3/19..	

DATE	EXPENSE CODE	DESCRIPTION	AMOUNT (ex VAT)	VAT	AMOUNT (inc VAT)
1 March	104	Taxi fare – office to Carlton Hotel & return			6.50
	112	Restaurant bill – Five Feathers Entertaining Mr Blythe & Mr Hinde of Databank Computers	76.09	11.41	87.50
2 March	101	Petrol – Bristol-Liverpool (185 miles @ 27.6p per mile)			42.56
	115	Hotel accommodation Waterloo Hotel Liverpool	32.50	4.88	38.38
3 March	101	Petrol – Liverpool-Bristol (185 miles @ 27.6p)			42.56
4 March	101	Petrol Bristol-Gloucester & return (72 miles @ 27.6 p)			19.87

CLAIMED BY: Ian Bretherton			111.59		237.37
AUTHORISED BY:		LESS ADVANCES PAID OUT:			—
		TOTAL AMOUNT DUE:			237.37

10 Draft the following letters:

a a letter of complaint to an organisation which consistently overcharges you on its invoices.

b a letter of apology to a firm where you have complained about an invoice being wrong (and made quite a fuss!) and then found out they were right after all!

You can add any details you need to make the letters more realistic.

Processing payments

Section 1 – Petty cash

Petty cash is the amount of money kept in the office to cover small day-to-day items of expenditure. The amount kept in petty cash is enough to cover expenditure for a week or a month. (The word 'petty' means small.)

Examples of petty cash expenditure

- A manager returns to the office from the station by taxi.
- The receptionist is told to buy flowers for the reception area.
- The milkman needs paying for milk delivered to the organisation.

Any employee who spends money on behalf of the organisation will obviously want paying back and this is done through petty cash.

THE IMPREST SYSTEM
This is the most widely used petty cash system.

- At the beginning of the petty cash period the petty cashier is issued with a float, or **imprest**, of an agreed amount, say £200.
- At the end of the period the total expenditure is calculated and balanced with the amount of money remaining.
- The petty cashier is then reimbursed with the money which has been spent, to restore the float to its original amount.

The petty cashier therefore starts every new petty cash period with the same imprest (float) amount.

The benefits of the imprest system

- It is easy to check.
- Expenditure is analysed.

- It limits outlay to a fixed sum.
- Sufficient money is always on hand.
- Increased demand for petty cash is quickly noticed and action can be taken (either by reducing expenditure or increasing the imprest.)
- It minimises work for the Chief Cashier.
- It links the petty cash system to the main Cash Book and accounts records.

The job of the petty cashier

Busy cashiers, in charge of thousands of pounds, do not want to be bothered with requests for small amounts of cash. It is therefore usual for a responsible member of staff to be put in charge of the petty cash float.

The petty cashier:

- is responsible for getting the float from the cashier initially
- keeps the money safely locked away in a strong petty cash tin
- makes sure that a petty cash voucher is completed every time money is spent. The voucher shows the reason for payment and is signed by the member of staff as they are repaid. The petty cashier also signs it to acknowledge it is correct and has been passed for payment

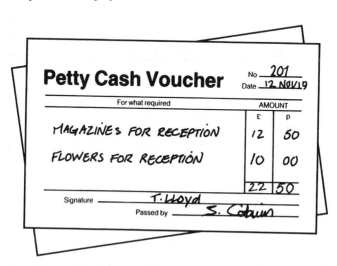

- attaches any official receipts, obtained by staff as proof of purchase, to the matching voucher
- sorts the vouchers into numerical order and enters these *daily* into the petty cash book. This book has analysis columns which correspond to the organisation's Ledger accounts. The different types of expenditure are therefore entered under a category heading, eg travel, stationery etc.
- files the vouchers in date and numerical order
- regularly checks to make sure that the total amount spent *plus* the amount of money remaining *equals* the amount of the original float
- balances the petty cash book at the end of the petty cash period and calculates the total amount spent on petty cash
- claims this money back from the chief cashier (who will usually check the petty cash book) so that the imprest is restored.

Security

- The petty cash tin should be
  - locked away when not in use
  - never left lying unattended.
- Strict control must be kept on the petty cash payments otherwise it is easy to lose small sums of money through loss or fraud.
- To help prevent fraud all vouchers *and* the petty cash book pages are *numbered*.
- When the vouchers are recorded into the petty cash book the number on the voucher is also entered. Any that are missing are therefore easily noticed.
- All vouchers *must* be passed or authorised before the money is paid out.
- The petty cash book is verified as correct by the chief cashier at regular intervals.

PETTY CASH AND VALUE ADDED TAX

Organisations which are registered for VAT can reclaim the money paid out in VAT on petty cash expenditure. To keep a record of this a separate VAT column is shown in most petty cash books.

For VAT to be reclaimed a VAT invoice *must* be obtained from the supplier. Only suppliers registered for VAT themselves can issue such an invoice. The invoice must show both the supplier's VAT Registration Number *and* the tax point of the invoice.

On a VAT invoice the amount, the item cost and the amount of VAT are usually shown separately. The price of the item is then entered in the petty cash book in the appropriate analysis column, the amount of VAT under the VAT column and the total amount spent in the total payments column.

Remember that *no* VAT is levied on travel (eg train fares, taxis etc), on food (except restaurant meals), books or magazines. The most common item in petty cash expenditure where VAT can be reclaimed is petrol. Garages usually issue VAT *inclusive* invoices or receipts so that the amount of VAT which has been paid must be worked out first.

VAT inclusive accounts

In some cases the amount paid on an account is *inclusive* of VAT, eg petrol. If an expense claim is submitted for a VAT inclusive item then the amount of VAT has to be calculated so that it can be recorded separately.

SPECIAL NOTE

Never 'guess' whether VAT should be listed separately. If you are in *any* doubt at all, *always* check with a supervisor.

CHECK IT YOURSELF

When you are at work or on work experience:

- find out the amount of petty cash kept by the company
- find out the main items of expenditure
- compare the type of voucher used with the example overleaf
- find out if your organisation is registered for VAT.

TEST YOURSELF

In each of the following cases a representative is claiming back money spent on petrol. Calculate the VAT in each case:

Mrs J Black	£16.50
Mr T Edmunds	£24.85
Mr L Malik	£17.20
Mrs M Walker	£29.40

Petty Cash Book example

Sarah Arshad is petty cashier at Merrivale Electronics. Her petty cash float is set at £400 per month. During February she passed vouchers for:

1 Feb	petrol	£15
3 Feb	coffee	£3.50
5 Feb	petrol	£45
8 Feb	visitor's buffet lunch	£52.25
8 Feb	return train ticket	£85.30
15 Feb	tea	£1.75
17 Feb	stationery	£27.00 + £4.05 VAT
19 Feb	art materials for display	£18.20 + £2.73 VAT
23 Feb	sandwiches	£14.75

The following shows her petty cash book for this month.

PETTY CASH BOOK

RECEIVED	DATE	FO	DETAILS	VCHR NO	TOTAL PAYMENTS	VAT	TRAVEL	BOOKS & STATIONERY	ENTERTAINING	OFFICE SUNDRIES
£400 00	1 FEB	CB12	BALANCE	b/d						
	"		PETROL	131	15·00	1.96	13.04			
	3 FEB		COFFEE	132	3·50					3.50
	5 FEB		PETROL	133	45·00	5·87	39.13			
	8 FEB		BUFFET LUNCH	134	52·25				52.25	
	"		RETURN TRAIN TICK.	135	85·30		85.30			
	15 FEB		TEA	136	1·75					1·75
	17 FEB		STATIONERY	137	31.05	4·05		27.00		
	19 FEB		ART MATERIALS	138	20·93	2·73				18.20
	23 FEB		SANDWICHES	139	14·75				14.75	
			TOTAL		269·53	14·61	137.47	27.00	67·00	23·45
			BALANCE c/d		130·47	GL6	GL10	GL23	GL31	GL63
£400·00					£400·00					
130·47	1 MARCH		BALANCE b/d							
269·53	"	CB12	CASH RECEIVED							

- Note the entry of each item under its appropriate analysis heading and the total column.
- VAT has been calculated on petrol and entered in the VAT column.
- The only other times VAT has been entered is where it was *specifically* listed.

BALANCING THE PETTY CASH BOOK

To balance the Petty Cash Book you must ensure that the following processes are carried out.

- All the analysis columns have been totalled.
- The total payments column is also totalled and this is cross-checked against the total of *all* the analysis columns and the VAT column added together.
- The balance carried down must equal the amount of money remaining at the end of the month.
- When the cashier restores the imprest this is also recorded.

CHECK IT YOURSELF
Work through this example carefully with your tutor. Make sure that you understand *every* entry and the way the balancing has been carried out at the end of the month.

TEST YOURSELF
You work as petty cashier for a company which is registered for VAT and are issued a float of £500 per month. Your vouchers for this month are

Date	Voucher No	Item	Cost
1 May	120	Coffee	£6.30
3 May	121	Papers	£3.50
5 May	122	Taxi	£14.50
8 May	123	Petrol	£32.50 (VAT inclusive)
10 May	124	Train fare	£63.00
15 May	125	Petrol	£36.70 (VAT inclusive)
18 May	126	Stationery	£43.70 + £5.70 VAT
23 May	127	Buffet	£47.20
27 May	128	Reference books	£37.50

Head your analysis columns as shown on the example. Draw up the petty cash book on 31 May and show the restoration of the cash to the imprest amount on 1 June.

SPECIAL NOTE

- Do remember to *cross-check* the total of all the analysis columns with the total payment column.
- If the figures don't balance then you will have to find your error. Do this *methodically* by:
  - counting all the entries to make sure you haven't missed one out
  - checking you have entered all the figures correctly
  - checking you have entered each item *twice* – once in the *correct* analysis column and once in the total payments column
  - checking that if the item contains VAT, the figure in the analysis column plus the VAT figure equals the total payment entry
  - checking your additions.

  Don't give up and ask for help without trying to find the error yourself!
- Use the example on page 44 to help you balance off correctly.
- Don't forget to carry down your new balance and add the money received to restore the imprest.

CHECK IT YOURSELF

Discuss with your tutor how you could systematically investigate a discrepancy between your final balance, and the amount of money remaining in the petty cash tin at the end of the month.

PETTY CASH AND THE MAIN ACCOUNTS

There is a close relationship between petty cash and the main accounts. Every organisation records payments in and out of the bank and payments made in cash in a **Cash Book**. Cash transferred to the Petty Cash Account is therefore entered as going *out* of the Cash Book (an entry on the credit side) and *in* to the Petty Cash Book (an entry on the debit side.) Note that you have been entering money received at the DR (debit) side of the Petty Cash Book.

At the end of the petty cash period, the total amount of expenditure under each analysis column must be posted to the correct expenses account in the General Ledger (eg Travel, etc.)

So that the system is easy to follow, **folio references** are used to indicate exactly where each amount of money has been posted from or posted to. This reference indicates the accounts book and page number, therefore CB12 would be Cash Book page 12, GL10 would mean General Ledger page 10. Often there is a separate folio column for this purpose.

Below is the same petty cash exercise which was used as an example on page 44. This time a folio column has been included and folio references written in. Note that these are written *underneath* the analysis columns where they refer to totals transferred to the General Ledger.

The Cash Book entry for the beginning of the month is also shown so that the relationship is easy to see.

DR	Cash £	Bank £	**Cash Book** 1 Feb Petty Cash	Cash £	Bank £ 400·00	Page12 CR

PETTY CASH BOOK

RECEIVED	DATE	FO	DETAILS	VCHR NO	TOTAL PAYMENTS	VAT	TRAVEL	BOOKS & STATIONERY	ENTERTAINING	OFFICE SUNDRIES
£400 00	1 FEB	CB12	BALANCE	b/d						
	"		PETROL	131	15·00	1·96	13·04			
	3 FEB		COFFEE	132	3·50					3·50
	5 FEB		PETROL	133	45·00	5·87	39·13			
	8 FEB		BUFFET LUNCH	134	52·25				52·25	
	"		RETURN TRAIN TICK.	135	85·30		85·30			
	15 FEB		TEA	136	1·75					1·75
	17 FEB		STATIONERY	137	31·05	4·05		27·00		
	19 FEB		ART MATERIALS	138	20·93	2·73				18·20
	23 FEB		SANDWICHES	139	14·75				14·75	
			TOTAL		269·53	14·61	137·47	27·00	67·00	23·45
			BALANCE	c/d	130·47	GL6	GL10	GL23	GL31	GL63
£400·00					£400·00					
130·47	1 MARCH		BALANCE	b/d						
269·53	"	CB12	CASH RECEIVED							

SECTION REVIEW

Having completed this section, you should now be able to:

1   List the duties of the petty cashier.

2   State the benefits of the imprest system and how this operates.

3   Withdraw money from the main cash account for the imprest.

4   Make payments from petty cash against correctly authorised vouchers.

5   Describe the relationship between VAT and petty cash.

6   Correctly enter petty cash expenditure into analysis columns, including expenses with VAT.

7   Accurately balance the petty cash book and reconcile cash held.

8   Describe the security procedures necessary in operating a petty cash system.

9   Explain the relationship between petty cash records and other accounts records.

REVIEW QUIZ

True or false?

1   Petty cash is for large items of expenditure.

2   At the end of a fixed period the petty cashier is reimbursed with the money which has been spent.

3   VAT is levied on all expenditure.

4   Vouchers are filed in alphabetical order.

5   Vouchers must be countersigned by the petty cashier when they are passed for payment.

Complete the blanks ...

6   The formula for calculating the VAT inclusive amount when VAT is 15% is ....

7   The total amount spent to date and the amount of money remaining must always equal ....

8 The system whereby the petty cash opening balance is the same at the start of each period is known as ....

Work it out

9 You are the petty cashier at Foyle Plastics Ltd. Your imprest is £500 per month.

Make out the Petty Cash Book for the month of April, using the following analysis columns (in addition to a VAT column):

Stationery   **Travel**   **Postage**   **Office Sundries**

You have been away ill for the past few weeks and, when you return, you find that your stand-in has not made any entries for the month. In addition, the vouchers are muddled up, both in terms of date and voucher number.

Sort out the voucher entries, shown below. Enter these correctly. Your organisation is registered for VAT so you should calculate how much VAT is involved in any petrol expenditure.

Balance off the petty cash book at the end of the month and restore the imprest on 1 May.

Date	Voucher No	Item	Cost
13 April	379	Plane ticket	£89.50
28 April	384	Window cleaning	£26.00
05 April	376	Charity donation	£15.00
16 April	380	Registered letter	£2.65
24 April	382	Petrol	£22.50
08 April	377	Plant for reception	£8.50
05 April	375	Stationery	£32.00 + £4.80 VAT
13 April	378	Train fare	£52.60
22 April	381	Coffee	£6.50
28 April	383	Telephone cleaning	£22.55 + £3.38 VAT

Section 2 – Receiving and recording payments

Organisations will receive payments in many different ways depending on the type of goods and services they provide.

The methods of payment used by customers will often depend on whether payment is made just once or over a period of time.

CHECK IT YOURSELF

What methods of payment do you think could be used:

• to buy goods in a retail store?
• to pay a doctor for a vaccination to go abroad?
• to buy a record advertised by a mail-order firm in a magazine?

TYPES OF PAYMENT

In all the above cases payment is only being made *once*. Therefore the most likely methods are cash, cheque, credit card or postal order – although not all would be acceptable in each case.

When something is being paid for over a long period of time, eg a car, a house or services such as electricity or gas, it is easier to use one of a range of services provided by the commercial banks.

All payments, whether they are received through the post, over the counter or via the banking system *must* be recorded accurately so that the information can be transferred to the correct accounts.

Mistakes can result in:

• annoyance, inconvenience and worry for customers
• a considerable amount of work for the accounts staff who have to find the error.

CASH PAYMENTS

All businesses which receive large amounts of cash daily use cash registers (tills) to record the payments and issue receipts. Every item is also printed automatically on an audit roll which is used to check every transaction through each cash register. A sales analysis can easily be achieved by allocating certain keys for certain types of sales and this is also printed on the record. The total for the day should obviously agree with the till return showing the money received. Any discrepancies should be noted and signed for by a senior member of staff, with the reason given, if known.

Technology update

The latest electronic cash registers:

- automatically calculate and display the change required
- are linked to the stock control system – the operator either keys in the stock number *or* uses a bar code reader to enter automatically the stock code
- fully itemise all purchases on the customer's receipt
- may automatically check credit cards and print individual sales vouchers
- can even print the name of the company and the amount of the payment on the customer's cheque.

 ## Handling cash

- You will usually be given a **float** in the morning. This is an amount of cash to enable you to give change easily even at the start of the day and will contain a mixture of coins (and maybe some notes). The amount of the float will vary, depending on the organisation.
- Check any money you receive *carefully* – watch out for foreign coins or tokens.
- *Always* count out the change to the customer. This acts as a check for them and a double check for you.
- If the till you are using does not calculate change automatically, place *notes* on the shelf above the till drawer (some tills have a special clip) whilst you get out the change. This prevents you forgetting whether the customer gave you a £5, £10 or £20 note – and also prevents anyone claiming to have given you a larger note than they actually did.

- If you are not using a till then the money received *must* be recorded on a payments inwards sheet. The design of this form will vary depending on why you are receiving the money.
- The total amount received during the day must be balanced with the total on the form or the till.

SPECIAL NOTE

The term **legal tender** means that the money is legally acceptable in payment. Scottish banknotes and Northern Ireland notes are both legal tender in England just as Bank of England notes are acceptable in those countries.

Technically, too large a quantity of coins can be refused as being not legal tender – more than £10 in 20p or 50p pieces, more than £5 in 10p or 5p coins and more than 20p in copper coins. In reality few organisations would refuse in case they lost a sale.

CHECK IT YOURSELF

Find out the largest denomination bank note issued by:

- the Bank of England
- the Bank of Scotland.

Written receipts

Customers who pay in cash often expect a receipt as proof of payment. Usually these are issued automatically by tills. Even in organisations which do not use a till it is usual to give a receipt – this time on a special form. Customers may specifically request a receipt, particularly if they wish to claim the money back from someone else.

The design of a receipt can vary. Small receipt books can be purchased with the headings printed on. Organisations may design their own to link to the type of payments being made.

SPECIAL NOTE

- Receipts designed to cope with large cash payments normally show the amount in *both* words and figures, as a double check.
- Receipts are always made out in *duplicate* so that the company also has a copy for its own records.

DUGDALE & YATES LTD

The Vehicle Bodyshop
Aberdare Road
CARDIFF
CD4 7JS

RECEIPT

No. **147** . . .

RECEIVED FROM ..... ᒐ *Donovan* ....

the sum of ..... *Thirty-two pounds* ....

.... | **£32·00** |

in payment of ..... *Replacement side window* ....

....

Received by ..... *Katherine Edwards* .... Date ... *14 May* .19—

PAYMENTS BY CHEQUE

There are *three* parties to any cheque:

- the **payee** – the person or company named on the cheque to receive the money
- the **drawee** – the bank from which the money is drawn
- the **drawer** – the person making out the cheque who will be drawing the money out of their account.

Crossed cheques

Today most cheques are printed with two vertical lines down the centre. This means the cheque is **crossed** and therefore *must* be paid into a bank account. It cannot be cashed over the counter and is therefore safer if it is lost or stolen.

> **CHECK IT YOURSELF**
> Study the example on page 54 and find the name of the drawee and the drawer and where the payee's name would be written. Identify the vertical lines which mean the cheque is crossed.

Note the different numbers printed on the cheque and why they are used.

Note the different numbers printed on the cheque and why they are used.

BARCLAYS BANK PLC	SPECIMEN

HIGH STREET, CAXTON, LONDON, N99 4XX   **29-99-93**   Bank sort code

Pay _____ or order

£

MR J & MRS ANN HARRIS

239535   299993   10329985

Cheque No   Bank sort code   Account No   Crossing lines

Checking cheques

Before accepting a cheque in payment the details must be checked carefully.

- The date must be accurate.
  - Early in a new year people often write the wrong year by mistake.
  - A cheque more than 6 months old is not valid.
  - *Never* accept a post-dated cheque – one made out for a later date than the date payment is being made.
- The payee's name must be correct. Many organisations have rubber stamps which they use to save the customer writing it in. In other cases the correct *official* title of the organisation is shown on a printed notice for people to copy.
- The amount in words and figures *must* agree.
- Any alterations must be initialled by the drawer.
- The signature must be the same as the specimen kept for that account by the bank. (See notes on cheque cards below.)
- The cheque should be written in blue or black ink.

SPECIAL NOTE

- The amounts should be written to the left of the lines to make alterations or additions difficult if not impossible.
- The amount of *pence* can be written in figures throughout.
- Any remaining blank spaces after the amount in words should be cancelled by drawing a line through them.

Cheque cards

Most private individuals are asked to produce a cheque card when they pay for goods by cheque. The amount on the card can vary, although the usual amount is £50. The card *guarantees* the cheque for the amount shown on the card.

When you are shown a cheque guarantee card you must check:

- the signature on the card – it must match that on the cheque
- the expiry date on the card – to check it is still valid
- the bank sort code on the card – it must match that on the cheque.

The cheque card serial number is then written clearly on the back of the cheque. Most organisations would also expect you to initial the back of the cheque too, and some organisations also ask for the customer's address.

SPECIAL NOTE

Many banks issue the same card for a variety of purposes, eg cash card, cheque card, debit card. The words *cheque guarantee* may therefore **not** appear on the front of the card you are offered, but on the reverse.

CREDIT CARD PAYMENTS

The most common credit cards in use today are **Access** and **Visa** cards. They are accepted by many organisations including garages, shops, restaurants and hotels and this fact is normally advertised in the window or near the counter.

If you are offered a credit card in payment you must check that the card is acceptable and seek authorisation when necessary. There are two ways of doing this.

Authorisation

The traditional method

All organisations have a **floor limit**. This is the maximum amount they can accept before they make a special check. The agreed floor limit may be as low as zero or as high as £500.

Above the floor limit a telephone call is made direct to the credit card company who run an immediate check through their computer to ensure the card hasn't been stolen and is not over the credit limit. If there are no problems they issue an **authorisation code** which is entered onto the voucher. This guarantees the payment.

The new method

The advent of new technology has meant considerable changes in the handling of credit cards:

- the card number is entered onto a special terminal linked to the credit card companies
- the card information is transmitted 'down the line' and automatically checked by computer
- if the check runs smoothly then a sales voucher is automatically printed by the terminal for signature by the card holder
- If the check shows a problem, eg that the card is stolen or the customer has exceeded his credit limit then a referral is made for further information and investigation. The method by which this is carried out may vary depending on the terminal used.

SPECIAL NOTE

Many organisations – especially retail stores – have their own sales vouchers for use with the normal credit cards *and* their own store cards. The information from these vouchers is extracted by the store and then transmitted electronically, rather than the vouchers themselves being processed.

Sales vouchers

Where sales vouchers are not issued automatically by a terminal, the sales vouchers for the appropriate credit card must be made out by hand.

The details from the credit card itself are transferred onto the voucher by means of a special imprinting machine.

The voucher is then completed by the sales clerk and the customer is asked to sign it. The signature *must* be checked with that on the card and the expiry date on the card must also be checked carefully. If you make a mistake destroy the voucher and start again – don't alter the shop copy – it *must* be identical to the customer's copy.

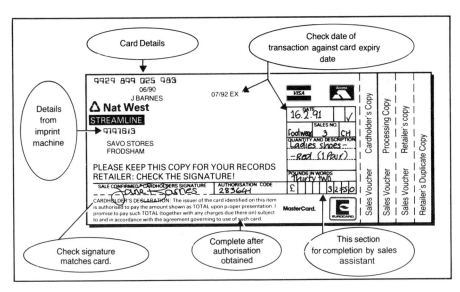

There are *four* copies of the sales voucher:

1 top copy – given to the customer
2 second copy – for the credit card company. This is paid into the bank
3 third and fourth copies – kept by the retailer (for at least 6 months).

Within 5 banking days of making out the vouchers, the company must complete a Voucher Summary Form which lists all the vouchers and take it and the vouchers to the bank for reimbursement.

It used to be the case that there was one type of voucher used for Visa transactions and a different type used for Access. Now retailers use a smaller type of sales voucher (see example above) for both types of transactions. This means there is only one voucher summary form to complete and all the vouchers – regardless of whether they are for Visa or Access cards – can be taken to the same bank.

 SPECIAL NOTE

- Under the new computerised terminal system there is no need for the retailer to deposit any vouchers at the bank. The top copy issued is given to the customer and the duplicate issued by the terminal is kept by the retailer. Because the credit card company computer has already checked and logged details of the transaction the money will be credited direct to the retailer's account.

- When credit card payments are being made by telephone, eg for theatre tickets, holiday deposits or mail order goods, the customer does not sign a voucher. The clerk receiving the call notes the customer's name and address, card number and the expiry date of the card. They can then carry out an acceptability check before issuing the goods or tickets. The voucher is usually sent by post as confirmation.

 TEST YOURSELF

1 The following customers each offer a £20 note in payment. How much would you give in change if they had bought goods worth

£6.47   £13.23   £19.20   £14.89   £11.96   £5.05?

2 How much money will you have received altogether if, in addition to the cash shown above, you have also received four cheques for £56.20, £18.03, £32.65 and £128.94?

 CHECK IT YOURSELF

Did you know that credit card companies *deduct* a percentage from the payment they make to retail organisations as their commission? Following a recommendation from the Monopolies and Mergers Commission organisations can now charge different prices, if they like, for goods bought by cash and goods bought by credit card.

- Do you think organisations will be more apt to *reduce* existing prices and offer discounts for cash or *increase* existing prices to charge extra for goods bought by credit card, and why?

> • Many organisations are against the idea of introducing a dual pricing system. Can you think why?

TECHNOLOGY UPDATE

A new option for paying is by **debit** card, eg Connect or cards under the Switch system. When these are put through a till linked to the EFTPOS* system the money is automatically transferred out of the holder's bank account and into the payee's bank account over the next three working days.

SPECIAL NOTE

It may be the case that you are asked for credit by a customer (ie he wants to take the goods and pay for them later) because:

- he hasn't enough money with him
- he has forgotten his cheque book or credit card
- he knows your boss well/has had credit before.

Never agree to anyone taking goods without paying without specific authorisation from your supervisor – no matter what the purchaser tells you!

RECORDING PAYMENTS RECEIVED

Payments received may be listed:

- by type of *payment* (cash, cheque, credit card)   *or*
- by type of *sale*.

PAYMENTS INWARDS ANALYSIS				
Date	Total Amount Received	By Cash	By Cheque	By Credit Card
4 March	16.50	16.50		
"	39.40		39.40	
"	8.00	8.00		
"	55.80			55.80
"	16.30		16.30	
"	73.00			73.00
"	21.80	21.80		
TOTALS	230.80	46.30	55.70	128.80

* **Electronic Funds Transfer at Point of Sale**

The listings may also include:

- remittances received through the post (though these may be recorded in a separate remittances book)
- payments made to service and delivery men or representatives, and brought into the office.

SECURITY

Organisations dealing with large amounts of cash have to take a variety of precautions:

- tills or cash drawers must be emptied *regularly*
- all money taken must be given to the cashier and locked in a properly mounted, fire-proof, wall or floor safe. (Some organisations have large 'walk-in' safes.)
- large organisations will have a safe which requires a minimum of *two* keyholders to open and lock it
- a burglar alarm will be fitted on the premises. This may have a direct line to the burglar alarm company who will contact the police if the alarm is activated
- staff who collect money when they are outside the premises, eg servicing staff, should *always* be required to give a numbered receipt to the customer
- staff who handle large amounts of cash should be vetted and their record-keeping checked
- large amounts of cash should not be kept on the premises overnight
- the company should be properly insured for any cash remaining on the premises.

CASHING UP

The correct way to cash up is to:

- separate cash and cheques
- list the cheques and add these up
- separate the bank notes according to denomination. Make sure the Queen's head is uppermost and to the right on each (they are easier to count this way)
- count the notes – first for £50, then £20, £10 and £5 and note down the amount *separately* for each denomination

- count pound coins into £10 piles – they should all be the same height! Put any coins left over alongside
- count 50p coins into £5 piles – again any left over should go alongside
- 20p coins are counted into £1 piles
- 10p and 5p coins can be mixed together – put into £1 units
- put 2p coins into piles of 10p *plus* 1p coins into piles of 10p
- total all the coins – again keeping denominations separate – £1 coins, 50p, 20p, remaining silver, all bronze coins.
- add the total of the cash received (notes plus coins)
- add to this the total of the cheques received.

SPECIAL NOTE

By dividing the notes and coins up in this way it is easy to double check your figures afterwards by counting *each* different denomination separately and ticking this off your list.

The final information is easy to transfer on to a bank paying-in slip.

Remember – Although you add up the number of coins (or notes) you list the **total** amount on your list – therefore 4 × £20 notes = £80.

TEST YOURSELF

How much altogether have you received if your cashing up results in

3 × £20 notes	6 × £10 notes	27 × £5 notes
16 × £1 coins	5 × 50p coins	19 × 20p coins
8 × 10p coins	19 × 5p coins	60p in bronze (2p and 1p coins)

SPECIAL NOTE

If you have opened with a float remember that this must be *deducted* from your total to find your net takings.

If your float this morning was £35 what are the net takings for the exercise above?

SECTION REVIEW

Having completed this section, you should now be able to:

1 Explain why all payments received must be recorded promptly and accurately.

2 Receive cash payments and count out correct change.

3   Cash up at the end of the working day and balance money received against takings and initial float issued.

4   Explain what is meant by the term **legal tender**.

5   Correctly complete receipts.

6   State which components on a cheque must be checked before it is accepted in payment.

7   Explain the function of a cheque card and the components which must be checked.

8   Accept payment by credit card, use the correct authorisation procedures and operate a credit card imprinter.

9   Differentiate between a debit card and a credit card and explain the term EFTPOS.

10   Explain how to deal with requests for credit.

11   List the security procedures to be followed when handling cash.

12   Explain the implications of different methods of payment.

REVIEW QUIZ

True or false?
1   Bank of Scotland notes can be spent in shops in England.

2   The drawee of a cheque is the person who signs it.

3   A cheque is no longer valid if it is over 3 months old.

4   The maximum amount of a cheque card is always £50.

5   The bank sort code appears twice on a cheque.

Complete the blanks ...
6   The term .... means that notes and coins can be used to buy goods in the normal way.

7   Two vertical lines drawn or printed on a cheque mean it is
     ....

8 A post-dated cheque is one which is ....

Work it out

9 Draw up a payments inwards sheet and list the following payments you have received today, under *type* of payment. Total the sheet and cross-check your figures.

By Cash – £13.85   £42.30   £2.45   £6.80   £9.76   £14.20

By Cheque – £34.80   £42.10   £113.80   £23.67   £50.02

By Credit Card – £34.50   £52.91   £102.56   £83.94

10 How much will you have taken altogether today if your cashing up results in:

6 × £50 notes	53 × £1 coins	29 × 5p coins
7 × £20 notes	17 × 50p coins	31 × 2p coins
23 × £10 notes	22 × 20p coins	16 × 1p coins
14 × £5 notes	19 × 10p coins	2 French francs

Section 3 – Routine banking transactions

DEPOSITING MONEY AT THE BANK

To avoid large sums of money being kept on the premises, takings should be banked regularly. A very large organisation may employ a special security company, eg Securicor, to transfer the money. Even a small organisation should bank their takings quickly and use the night safe if the bank has closed by the time they have cashed up. Any cash left on the premises must be locked away in the safe.

SPECIAL NOTE

Organisations with cash registers usually leave the till drawers *open* at night (and obviously empty) to prevent them being forced open if there is a break-in.

Transporting money

- Cash should be placed in special plastic bank bags before being taken to the bank. The bags are different colours and hold different denominations of coins (eg £20 in £1 coins). It does not matter if the bags aren't full but banks object strongly to bags containing mixed coins.

- Staff should *never* be asked to carry large amounts of cash to the bank – especially on a regular basis. If you *are* asked to do so (and it would create problems to refuse) then the very least you should insist on is someone to accompany you.
- If you regularly take small amounts of money to the bank then vary your route and the time at which you go.

Bank procedure

The bank will check the amount of money you hand over – they count notes and weigh bags of coins.

They will tick each entry on the paying-in slip (for details see below) as they check it.

If all is correct they will initial both the paying-in slip and the counterfoil (or duplicate) and date stamp it. Do check this is done (banks do make mistakes!). The cashier will keep the top copy of the paying-in slip and return the book to you.

If there is a minor discrepancy the cashier will ask if you agree this and then amend your paying-in slip accordingly. If the error is a major one, you will be given everything back to sort out yourself.

SPECIAL NOTE

- When money is being cashed up and a paying-in slip prepared, cheques and postal orders should be *re-checked* to make sure they are completed properly and not out-of-date.
- *Don't* try to pay any foreign coins into the bank – they will be rejected. If you accept any in error it is your loss.

CHECK IT YOURSELF

- Money can now be paid into the bank at automated deposit machines. These are usually situated *inside* the bank and are useful if the counters are very busy. See if you can see one in your local branch and watch it being used.
- See if you can see the night safe at your local bank. Find out the procedure for companies who wish to use this facility.

Paying-in slips

Whenever money is taken to a bank a paying-in slip is completed. This lists the payments received, divided into cash and cheques.

On the back of each paying-in slip there is space to list the drawers of cheques and the amount of each cheque. The total of this is carried forward to the front and added to the cash total. A *separate* list of all cheques should also be kept by the company in case there are any queries.

The cash must be analysed, ie divided into different denominations. The example below has been completed by a cashier who had the following:

2 × £50 notes	7 × £1 coins	17 × 5p coins
7 × £20 notes	11 × 50p coins	17 × 2p coins
6 × £10 notes	7 × 20p coins	12 × 1p coins
23 × £5 notes	9 × 10p coins	

In addition the cheques have been listed on the reverse and the total carried forward. (Postal orders are also listed with cheques – in exactly the same way.)

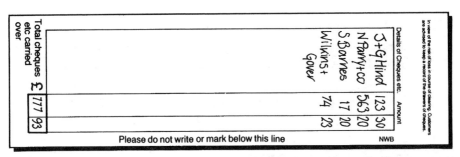

Complete a paying in slip for your company, JTS Services Ltd, and date it today. Your takings are:

2 cheques – £183.45 (Mrs A Brand) £63.40 (Mr B Henry); 1 postal order – £40.50 (Miss S Walker)

Cash –		
1 × £50 note	13 × £1 coins	15 × 5p coins
15 × £20 notes	22 × 50p coins	13 × 2p coins
5 × £10 notes	17 × 20p coins	3 × 1p coins
16 × £5 notes	6 × 10p coins	

! SPECIAL NOTE

- If you make a mess of a paying-in slip (eg when working out your cash analysis), *don't* take it to the bank. Cancel it clearly and neatly write out another one.
- Paying in credit card vouchers and making out a voucher summary form are dealt with on pages 56–7.

WITHDRAWING CASH FROM THE BANK

Private individuals can take money out of their accounts by:

- cashing a cheque
- using the cash machine.

Cash machines are in service 24-hours a day and, in addition to obtaining cash, users can order a statement, a new cheque book or ask for the balance of their account.

Each user is given a **PIN** (personal identification number) which he or she must *remember* and not write down! In addition the user will be issued with a cash card. Some banks *combine* cheque cards and cash cards together now.

Each cash card holder has a maximum limit for each day or week and requests outside this limit (or if there is no money in the account) will be refused.

Cashing a cheque

If a cheque is being cashed then the word 'cash' is substituted for the name of the payee, as in the example below.

Note the wording that has been written *sideways* on the cheque, through the two vertical lines.

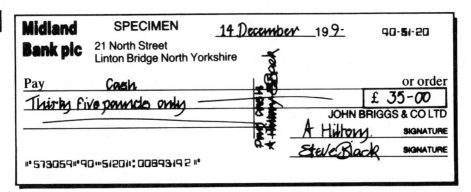

The two vertical lines printed on a cheque mean the cheque is **crossed**. A crossed cheque is safer than one which is not crossed because it *must* be paid into a bank account and cannot be cashed. Whilst this is normally better (if a cheque was lost nobody could obtain cash for it) it prevents cash being obtained. To change this situation the crossing has to be cancelled and the cheque **opened**.

This is done by writing the words *pay cash* and adding the signature of the drawer *inside* the crossing.

SPECIAL NOTE

Many banks still do not like this method as there is obviously a risk of fraud or the wrong person obtaining cash. They will prefer a cheque to be made out to the person concerned (the payee) and then the cheque 'opening' in the same way. The payee must provide evidence of identity at the bank.

Cash may be required for a till float, petty cash or to pay wages. In each case certain denominations of coins will be required – a till float of £25 is useless if it comprises 2 × £10 notes and 1 × £5 note!

CHECK IT YOURSELF

Assume you have to obtain £30 in cash as a till float. How many coins of each denomination would you choose so that you will be able to give change easily at the beginning of the day? Discuss your answer with your tutor.

FOREIGN CURRENCY

In addition to exchanging cheques for British currency, you may have to cash a cheque to buy foreign currency if someone is travelling abroad. Banks usually need prior notification of foreign currency requirements – especially if the amount required is large or the currency is one which is not often requested. Beware too, that some countries have restrictions on the amount of foreign currency which can be taken into the country.

Follow the procedures listed below when obtaining currency for foreign travel.

1 Telephone the bank and tell them your request – if possible at least 7 days before you will need the money.

2 Check there are no restrictions on the amount you are requesting.

3 You can ask the bank if you can receive the money in certain denominations, eg 6 × $50 bills not 3 × $100 bills – but you may be told that you have to accept what is sent!

4 Find out the approximate exchange rate and the bank commission so that you can given this information to your Chief Cashier, if required.

5 On the day you are collecting the money, telephone the bank first to find out the exact amount your cheque must be made out for. This will depend on the exchange rate in operation on the day the bank actually obtained the currency for you.

6 Make out the cheque for the specified amount, have it signed and take it to the bank.

7 Check that the calculations on the bank form you are given are correct in terms of the currency you have received and the amount you have paid for it.

Checking currency calculations

A bank form will have headings similar to those shown below:

Country	Currency Amount	Rate	Sterling Equivalent	Commission	Net Sterling
France	5850	9.8	596.94	1.80	598.74

SECTION REVIEW

Having completed this section, you should now be able to:

1 Explain the security measures which should be taken when taking money to the bank.

2 Correctly analyse cash and complete a bank paying-in slip including cash, cheques and postal orders.

3 Explain the common errors which may occur and how these should be rectified.

4 Pay in cash, cheques and postal orders at the bank.

5 Cash a cheque for British or foreign currency.

6 Check the amount of foreign currency against the sterling equivalent and net amount required.

REVIEW QUIZ

True or false?

1 Coins must be analysed into denominations before a paying-in slip is completed.

2 PIN stands for proper identity number.

3 Takings should be banked at the same time every day.

4 Foreign coins are not accepted by a bank.

5 To cash a cheque all you have to do is to write 'cash' instead of the payee's name.

Complete the blanks ...

6 Try to notify the bank of foreign currency requirements ...... days in advance.

7 Bags should never contain .... coins.

8 Banks prefer an 'opened' cheque to be made out to a .... rather than made out for cash.

Work it out

9 Make out a bank paying-in slip, dated today, for the following:

2 cheques – Mr T Wood – £189.52, Ms C Bonham – £532.90

2 postal orders – Mr G Sulaman – £18.60, Miss J. O'Connell – £60.28

Cash – 3 × £50 notes   38 × £1 coins   13 × 10p coins
         6 × £20 notes   11 × 50p coins   23 × 2p coins
         5 × £5 notes   14 × 20p coins   2 × 1p coins

10 a What figures should be entered into the blank columns on the form below?

    b What should be the total amount of your cheque?

    c Can you find out the name of the currency for each country given below?

Country	Currency Amount	Rate	Sterling Equivalent	£ Commission	Net Sterling
Germany	1160	2.90		1.70	
France	7776	9.72		1.70	
USA	1196.92	1.84		1.70	
Belgium	31065.72	59.65		1.70	
Holland	1159.35	3.275		1.70	

Section 4 – Making payments to suppliers and others

In business most suppliers are paid by cheque:

- after any invoices have been carefully checked and passed for payment
- after the statement has been received at month end showing the total amount due for that month
- after the statement has been checked to make sure that all invoices, credit notes and payments to date have been included and calculated correctly.

INVOICES, CREDIT NOTES AND STATEMENTS

Invoices

Invoices are issued by suppliers detailing the goods which have been despatched, the price, VAT charges, any discounts and the total amount due. All invoices must be carefully checked before they are passed for payment.

If an organisation undercharges for an item a Supplementary Invoice will be sent, detailing the additional amount due.

Credit notes

Credit notes are issued when the buyer has been overcharged. This may be because of an error on the invoice or because some goods were returned to the supplier, eg because they were faulty.

Statements

At the end of the month the supplier issues a statement. This shows:

- the balance which was owing at the beginning of the month
- any invoices which have been issued during the month
- any credit notes which have been issued during the month
- any payments which have been received during the month
- the new balance.

SPECIAL NOTE

- The debit column shows amounts owing to the supplier.
- The credit column shows deductions from this, eg payments and credit notes.
- The balance column is completed after each transaction.

Checking the documents

You will probably already have had experience in checking invoices. Credit notes must be checked to make sure that the price and discounts for the goods match those on the invoice.

Statements must be checked to make sure no payment, invoice or credit note has been omitted.

All documents should be checked to make sure that the
calculations are correct *before* any cheque is made out in payment.

		Number	200/689	
		Date	30 April 19–	

S T A T E M E N T

Browns of Bath
14 Crescent Parade
Bath
BT3 4PS

VAT Registration Number
209/48927/62

TO: P Robinson & Co Ltd

14 Spa Road

CHELTENHAM   CL3 9DS

Account No   3920/TM

Date	Particulars	Debit	Credit	Balance
1 April	Balance			£702.00
3 April	Invoice S27320	£200.00		£902.00
7 April	Invoice S27389	£102.68		£1002.68
10 April	Cheque		£702.00	£300.68
14 April	Credit Note CR68		£200.00	£500.68
18 April	Invoice S 28372	£350.00		£850.68
24 April	Credit Note CR89		£62.50	£788.18
28 April	Invoice S 29378	£250.00		£1038.18
29 April	Credit Note CR95	£100.00		£938.18

TEST YOURSELF

1 Why did P Robinson pay £702 on 10 April?
2 Test your checking skills! There are 4 errors in the statement above – can
you find them and state the correct amount owing to Browns at the end of the
month?

SPECIAL NOTE

On some accounts the buyer is offered a cash discount if he pays promptly.
Unless your organisation operates a different procedure, such payments must be
made whilst the option for the discount is still in force, so that the lower amount
can be paid.

TEST YOURSELF

1 Make out cheques in payment of two accounts. One for £149.65 to Midvale
Office Suppliers and one for £69 to Copyrite Ltd. Date both with today's
date but *do not sign them*. (If you have forgotten how to write cheques, look
back at page 54.)
2 You have received an account from the local florist, who is not registered for
VAT, for £25.00 less 2½% discount if the account is paid in 10 days. What is
the amount due if you pay promptly?

TEST YOURSELF

You have received three accounts – all of which offer discount if paid promptly. All the companies are registered for VAT. What is the amount due on each one if a) you pay immediately b) you pay after the cash discount option has expired? (Remember the VAT figure does not change.)

1   Superware Ltd   £145.60 – 10% trade discount – 5% cash discount if paid in 10 days + VAT
2   Coleman & Green Ltd   £527.00 – 5% trade discount – 2½% cash discount if paid in 14 days + VAT
3   Cookham Travel Ltd   £228.50 – 7½% cash discount if paid in 7 days + VAT.

AUTHORISATION PROCEDURES

The authorisation procedures vary from one organisation to another and will also vary depending on the amount of the payment. Obviously there are stricter regulations governing the payment of large amounts, eg

- up to £200 one authorised signature is required on the cheque
- between £200 and £1000 two authorised signatures are required (one a director)
- £1000 to £10000 requires two directors' signatures
- above £10000 authorisation also required by the Managing Director.

Note that the above is only an example of an authorisation procedure – it is important that you check the actual procedure in force in any organisation where you are responsible for making payments.

PAYING ACCOUNTS

It is not usual to simply put a cheque in an envelope and send it off! If this was done the organisation receiving it would not know what the cheque was for without referring to its accounts.

For this reason it is usual to enclose a **remittance advice** with all cheques, stating the reason for payment.

You may find that a remittance advice is included as a tear-off form on an invoice you receive. In this case you can simply detach the form and return it with the cheque. Companies often issue invoices like this so that they can easily identify cheque payments received from private individuals.

Most business organisations, however, have their own remittance advice forms, as shown below.

```
T ROSS LTD                           REMITTANCE ADVICE

Craiglands Industrial Estate
                                     ────────────────
EXETER   5EX 9PF
                                     YOUR INV    4893/SL
┌                    ┐
                                     INV   AMT   £423.89
  Booth & Walker Ltd
  14 Maritime Way                    OUR   REF   OFF/2110
  TORQUAY
  TR4 7DM                            ┌──────────────────────────────┐
└                    ┘               │ TOTAL VALUE OF CHEQUE  £423.89 │
                                     └──────────────────────────────┘

  DATE:   19 May 199–        CREDITOR NO:   0952  CHEQUE NO 001291
```

 ## SPECIAL NOTE

The four small marks around the name and address of the creditor denote where the address must be typed or printed so that the remittance advice can go in a window envelope with the cheque behind it. This saves the Accounts Department having to type an ordinary envelope.

Technology update

Many organisations today produce all their accounts on computer. A remittance advice would therefore be printed automatically when payment was being made. The computer can also be used to print out the cheques automatically and these can then be transferred to a cheque signing machine for automatic printing of signatures.

This system is only likely to be used in large organisations paying hundreds or thousands of cheques each month. Obviously such a machine is kept under lock and key when not in use and strictly supervised when in use.

Other types of notification

An organisation which pays out refunds on a fairly regular basis may have a standard letter printed to accompany such cheques. In this case only the variables would be completed when a refund is made. Most large holiday operators use this type of standard letter.

TEST YOURSELF

Assume you work for a large holiday booking agent. You have been asked to compose a short, standard letter to accompany any refund cheques. In addition to the basic text of the letter there should be space for:

- holiday booking reference
- amount of cheque
- passenger name(s)
- departure date
- cheque number
- reason for refund
- destination
- refund reference number.

Design and write a suitable letter and check the contents with your tutor. Then type it on a word processor and think up details to complete three letters to different clients.

Paying out cash

Cash payments may be made in certain circumstances, ie to employees reclaiming their expenses. If you are involved in making cash payments:

- ask for identification unless you know the person well
- make sure the person receiving the money signs for it
- count out the money – as a double check to both yourself and the recipient.

Don't pay money to one person on another person's behalf unless you are expressly instructed to do so by your supervisor. You must always make sure that the person who is being paid the money is the one who is authorised to receive it.

Other payments

In the same way that private individuals do not pay all their accounts by cheque, neither do businesses. In some cases they may take advantage of the wide variety of bank services available.

BANK PAYMENT SERVICES

There are a variety of bank services where money is transferred through the banking system from one account to another.

CHECK IT YOURSELF

Look at the bottom of any type of bill you or your parents receive regularly, eg gas, electricity, telephone, water rates etc. Here you will see a special printed form with the words Bank Giro Credit at the top, similar to the one shown below.

G Girobank Trans Cash	**TELECOM**	Payment Counterfoil	**Bank Giro Credit**
Girobank plc Bootle Merseyside GIR 0AA			By transfer from Girobank a/c no
Customer account number	Credit account number	Amount due	
155 205 285	2736 2036	616 9082	£ 54.18	
Cashier's stamp and initials		No fee payable at PO counter Cheque acceptable	
	Signature	Date	
		16 – 90 – 82	Cash
		The Royal Bank of Scotland plc Head office Collection Account	Cheques
No. of Fee Cheques	**LANCS & CUMBRIA**	British Telecommunications plc Lancs and Cumbria District Please do not fold this counterfoil or mark or write below this line	TOTAL £

```
      MR  T K EDDLESTON
      15 LAKESIDE DRIVE
      WINDERMERE
      WM3 9AQ
```

Bank giro credit

If you complete a Bank Giro Credit form and take it to the bank –
together with your cheque or cash for the amount stated – the
bank will automatically transfer the money to the account stated
on the form – on page 76 to British Telecom Account 6169082.
It doesn't matter where in the country this account is held.

Standing orders

An alternative method which bank account holders can use to
transfer money from one account to another is by **standing
order**. The standing order form instructs the bank to transfer a
fixed amount of money at regular intervals to another account. It
is used to pay mortgages, insurance premiums or subscriptions.

The form gives all the details of the payee's account. See example
on page 78.

Direct debit

Although the standing order system saves the customer the
trouble of having to keep posting cheques to an organisation, if
the amount of money to be paid changes, or if the payments are
not made regularly then it can be inconvenient to keep having to
notify the bank of the changes.

Therefore, in cases where payments are likely to vary from one
period to another it is more usual for bank customers to use the
direct debit system.

PART TWO: INSTRUCTIONS TO YOUR BANK TO PAY DIRECT DEBITS

(Full postal address)
To: The manager _MIDLAND_ _____ Bank
MARKET STREET
ABERDEEN ___ Postcode _____

- I instruct you to pay Direct Debits from my account at the request of Guardian Royal Exchange Assurance plc.
- The amounts are fixed and are to be debited on various dates.
- I understand that Guardian Royal Exchange Assurance plc may change the amounts and dates only after giving me prior notice.
- I will inform the Bank in writing if I wish to cancel this Instruction.
- I understand that if any Direct Debit is paid which breaks the terms of this instruction, the Bank will make a refund.

Bank or Giro Account No. `3 0 4 9 8 2 6 5 0`

Bank Sort Code (see top right hand corner of your cheque book) `4 0` – `2 0` – `1 8`

Name(s) of Account Holder(s)
Miss JANE HOWARTH

Note for Bank
Correspondence about this instruction should be sent to: Guardian Royal Exchange, Life Accounts Dept, Ballam Road, Lytham St Annes, FY8 4JZ.

Signature(s) _Jane Howarth_

Date _15/1/99_

Banks may refuse to accept instructions to pay Direct Debits from some types of account

Facts about Direct Debiting
Direct Debiting is a simple, inexpensive and convenient way of paying your premium. All you need to do is sign and return the instruction which authorises your Bank to debit your account when your premiums are payable. The processing of the instruction may result in some delay in collecting the first premium(s). Such delay will never exceed three months and does not affect your rights under the policy. The payment date(s) will be determined by GRE when your application is accepted. The instruction has been designed so that you do not have to enter the amount of your premium. No collection of premium will be made before it is due and the amount collected will be stated in your policy. If GRE should request payment in error, you may seek immediate reimbursement from GRE through your Bankers under an indemnity lodged in their favour by GRE. You may cancel your Direct Debit Instruction at any time by notifying your Bank and GRE accordingly.

`9 9 0 4 9 1`

Direct debit forms are printed by the organisation for its customers, *not* by the bank. The organisation sends this form to customers who may be interested in paying by direct debit. The customer completes it, returns it to the organisation and they then forward it to the bank.

The form authorises the customer's bank to pay the organisation from the customer's account as required.

TEST YOURSELF

1 From the details shown on the standing order form, how much will Jane Howarth pay her insurance company in total next year?

2 What advantages do you think there are in using the standing order system?

3 Can you think of any disadvantages?

4 Compare the standing order with the direct debit on page 77.

To ✖ The Royal Bank of Scotland plc	Standing Order

Please make the payments detailed below and debit my/our   Current account

Name of A/c to be debited __Jane P Howarth__   A/c No __0649 2100__

Reference No to be quoted __HO/TD/4831__   Date __15 Jan 199-__
(if any)

Name of Payee __Grampian insurance co__   A/c No __42 736814__

Address of Payee __Thistle Street__
__Edinburgh EH1 7JE__

Bank & Branch to which __National Westminster Bank__ Code No __60-01-01__
payment is to be made __Ainsle Street__
__Edinburgh EH3 4PT__

Amount (in words) __FIFTEEN POUNDS__

£ __1500__

Date of payments __Second of each month__

Date of first payment __2 Feb 199-__

Special instructions (if any) __—__

* Payments are to continue until __FURTHER NOTIFICATION__

* Payments are to continue until you receive further notice in writing
This instruction cancels any previous order in favour of the Payee named above under this reference.

Signature __June Howarth__

* Delete as necessary
04805 (9/84)

Security

Only recognised organisations are allowed to submit direct debit mandates to banks, eg electricity and gas boards, insurance companies and building societies etc. This prevents any 'cowboy' operators helping themselves to money from customers' accounts when they wish! The organisation *must* notify the customer if the payment details change.

TEST YOURSELF

List the advantages of using the direct debit system rather than standing order.

Credit transfer

When employees start working for an organisation they have the option of being paid in cash, by cheque or by credit transfer. If they choose credit transfer then their wages or salary will be paid directly into their bank account each week or month.

TRANSFERRING MONEY – AT HOME . . . . . .

CHAPS

CHAPS stands for Clearing House Automated Payment System and this is used by all the banks to transfer money for their clients quickly across the country. The main High Street banks are linked to CHAPS via computer and the information is merely keyed in at one branch and relayed onwards to the receiving bank by CHAPS.

. . . . . . AND ABROAD

Eurocheque

Holders of Eurocheque books can make out a Eurocheque in any currency and send this abroad to pay for goods. Note – more and more countries are joining the Eurocheque system – it is *not* just restricted to countries such as France and Spain, which are geographically situated in Europe.

Standard transfer or urgent transfer

These are computerised methods of transferring funds abroad – the urgent method costs slightly more but is quicker. The service operates to any country in the world. The customer specifies the payee, his bank and the amount to be paid. The British bank then contacts (by computer) the nearest correspondent bank abroad to where the money is to be paid. The correspondent bank then relays the money onwards.

TEST YOURSELF

From what you have read on bank payment services, which service would you recommend in each of the following cases?

1 To pay business insurance premiums to the insurance company.
2 To pay staff salaries.
3 A solicitor wishes to send his client's deposit for a house urgently across the country.
4 To pay the deposit on a hotel booking in the south of France.

SECTION REVIEW

Having completed this section, you should now be able to:

1 Check payment requests for accuracy and authorisation.

2 Identify discrepancies and errors on statements of account.

3 Explain how invoices, credit notes and payments made are calculated on the statement of account to give the balance owing.

4 Complete cheques accurately.

5 Complete remittance advice forms.

6 Describe the circumstances under which payment must be made promptly.

7 Calculate discounts and VAT.

8 List the procedure to follow when paying out cash.

9 State the main bank payment services and why they are used.

10 Explain how authorisation procedures may differ between small and large payments

True or false?

1 Cash discounts are offered to encourage prompt payment.

2 Credit notes are issued when the buyer has been overcharged.

3 Statements are issued at the beginning of each month.

4 Eurocheques can only be used for countries situated within Europe.

5 A direct debit can only be used to pay a fixed sum of money at regular intervals.

Complete the blanks . . .

6 A person claiming a cash payment should be asked for
. . . .

7 The form which is sent to accompany cheques in payment is called a . . . .

8 Completed direct debit forms are sent to the . . . .

Work it out

9 You have received a statement from Daniel & Sons, of Wolverhampton. According to your records the balance at the start of the month is correct. This month:

- you have paid them 3 cheques for £132, £300.20 and £42.18.

- you have received goods on 3 occasions. The invoice details are as follows:

  Invoice S 58279 £223.59 – 10% trade discount + VAT

  Invoice S 62892 £816.42 – 10% trade discount + VAT

  Invoice S 70982 £230.80 – 10% trade discount + VAT (this was a special order subject to 2½ discount if you pay it within 14 days)

- You also returned goods once and received a credit note CR542. The goods returned were valued at £32 and the terms of payment were as shown on Invoice S 58279.

Check the statement below carefully against the above transactions and check all the calculations.

Correct any errors you find and make a note of these for your supervisor.

STATEMENT		**Number** 428637		
		Date 30 June 199–		
Daniel & Sons		**VAT Registration Number**		
22 Ainsley Park Wolverhampton WV4 8LR		293/273648/73		
TO: Markham & Ellis Ltd		**Account No** 6342		
14 Priory Walk				
SHREWSBURY SW2 1JP				

Date	Particulars	Debit	Credit	Balance
1 June	Balance			£489.00
3 June	Cheque		£132.00	£621.00
9 June	Cheque		£300.00	£321.00
15 June	Invoice S 58279	£231.42		£552.42
19 June	Credit Note CR 542		£36.80	£515.62
24 June	Invoice S 62892	£929.70		£1145.32
28 June	Cheque	£42.18		£1487.50
30 June	Invoice S 70982	£232.90		£1720.40

10   Make out a cheque for the correct amount to Daniel & Sons and complete a Remittance Advice form to be sent with it.

Processing payroll

PAYMENTS
Employees in an organisation are either paid a **wage** or a **salary**.

- **Wages** are paid weekly, often on a Friday.
- **Salaries** are paid monthly – either every four weeks (13 times a year) or, more usually, every calendar month (12 times a year).

Wages
Production and manual workers are usually paid each week. Although employees no longer have the right to insist on being paid in cash, many weekly wages are still paid this way.

The worker may be paid:

- **flat rate** – the same sum of money each week
- **time rate** (also called hourly rate or basic rate). In this case the hourly rate is multiplied by the number of hours worked. Higher rates are paid for overtime
- **piecework** – the worker is paid for the amount of work carried out – the harder the person works the more pay is received. The problem with this system is that in the rush to earn good money the quality of the work may be poor.

Salaries
Clerical and office staff are usually salaried and paid once a month. They are more likely to be paid by cheque or credit transfer than by cash.

Employees who are paid by credit transfer (see page 113) receive a salary slip at the end of the month giving details of their pay and deductions.

Other payments
- **commission** may be paid either
  - on top of a basic salary. This method is often used to pay

sales staff – the more they sell, the higher their commission.

– at a high rate *instead* of a wage or salary. Such earnings can obviously not be relied upon as in a bad week nothing will be earned.

- **bonus** payments may be paid to staff as a reward for greater productivity or extra effort at a busy time of year, eg Christmas.
- **profit sharing** is organised by some companies. Employees receive a share in any profits made.
- **expenses** – strictly speaking these are not really methods of payment as the employee might only be being reimbursed for money he has already spent (eg on petrol or entertaining) – see section on expense claims.

Perks or fringe benefits

Some companies also give certain perks to their employees. These often depend on where the company is situated, the business it is in, and the job held by the employee. The most obvious is a company car but many retail organisations, for example, sell goods at discount to their employees.

CHECK IT YOURSELF

At your work place or the organisation you visit on work experience, try to find out:

- how many employees are paid weekly on an hourly rate
- if any employees are paid weekly on a flat rate
- how many employees are paid monthly
- if the employees receive any perks in addition to their normal pay.

Compare any perks you are told about with other members of your group. Discuss the type of perks offered by companies with your tutor and how much you think they are worth in addition to salary.

RECORDING TIME WORKED

Many workers are paid according to the number of hours they have worked. It is therefore essential that a strict record is kept of the time each employee starts and ends work each day.

Financial Administration: Specialist Units

This is particularly important for:

- hourly paid employees
- those working flexitime.

Today most clocking in and out systems are computerised. Each employee has his or her own key or card to insert into the machine. A visual display then displays the hours worked (as a check to the employee) and relays the information direct to a computer.

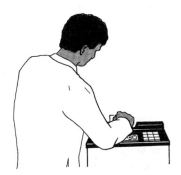

In other organisations 'time cards' are still used where a hole is punched in a column to record late arrivals or early departures. Some organisations operating flexitime merely have an attendance book which has to be signed on arrival and counter-signed by someone in authority.

SPECIAL NOTE

One of the most serious offences which can be committed by any member of staff is to clock another employee in or out. In many organisations this is punishable by instant dismissal.

Calculating hours worked

If the wages are not automatically calculated by computer then it is the job of the wages clerk to use the clock (or time) cards to work out the **gross pay** for each worker. This is the amount paid *before* any deductions are made.

The wages clerk has to take into consideration not only hours worked at basic rate but also any hours worked at overtime rates, eg time and a quarter, time and a half or double time.

Time and a quarter is simply the basic rate plus a quarter as much again. Therefore an employee paid £4 per hour would receive £5.

Similarly time and a half is the basic rate plus half as much again (£6) and double time is twice the normal rate (£8).

TEST YOURSELF

How much would each of the following be paid for time and a quarter, time and a half and double time?

Name	Basic Rate	Name	Basic Rate
Raymond Black	£3.60	Graham Poole	£2.95
Jonathan Small	£5.20	Martin Aspin	£4.95
Susan Wells	£4.16	Colin Browne	£7.25

SPECIAL NOTE

Don't forget to round off your answers to two decimal places. It is worth noting that most organisations round *up* rates for wage payments – therefore £2.25 at time and a quarter = £2.82 not £2.81.

Understanding clock cards

Although computerised clocking in systems can automatically distinguish between normal time, normal overtime and special overtime and calculate the number of hours worked at each rate, other machines still print the time of arrival and departure and the wages clerk has to calculate hours worked at each rate.

Lateness (and other discrepancies) are usually printed in red and many organisations make deductions for more than a specified number of minutes lateness either per day or per week.
A clock card for an hourly paid employee is shown opposite.

TEST YOURSELF

Hanif Patel is paid £4.80 per hour for a 38 hour week. Overtime on weekdays is paid at time and a quarter for the first six hours and time and a half after that. Sunday overtime is paid at double time. Last week, in addition to his normal hours, he worked an extra 10 hours during the evening and 3 hours on Sunday.

What is his gross wage for the week?

CHECK IT YOURSELF

On the example shown below, Janice Thompson is employed to work a basic 37½ hour week at £5 per hour. Overtime on weekdays is paid at time and a quarter for the first 5 hours and time and a half after that. Saturday overtime is time and a half and Sunday working is paid at double time.

A total of 15 minutes lost time for lateness is allowed per week before any deductions are made.

WORKS NO 428	NAME Janice P Thompson WEEK ENDING 4 May 19–							STANDARD WEEK HRS 37½	
		MON	TUES	WED	THUR	FRI	SAT	SUN	
IN		0800	0758	**0810**	0759	0759		0900	
OUT		1200	1200	1200	1200	1200		1200	
IN		1300	1300	1300	**1303**	1300			
OUT		1630	1730	1630	1630	1630			
IN				1700	1700				
OUT				2000	2030			TOTALS	
LOST TIME				·10	·03				·13
TOTAL ORD		7·30	7·30	7·20	7·27	7·30			37·17
TOTAL 1¼		1		3	1				5
TOTAL 1½					2·30				2·30
TOTAL 2								3	3

Late arrival in bold

Total lost time and ordinary time must equal standard week hours

	No of Hrs	Rate	Earnings
Ord Time	37½	5·00	187·50
Time + 1¼	5	6·25	31·25
Time + 1½	2½	7·50	18·75
Double Time	3	10·00	30·00
		GROSS PAY £	267·50

Work through the card carefully yourself. Identify:
- the times she clocked in and out each day
- that her lost time does *not* exceed the 15 minutes allowed each week so no deductions have been made from her basic pay
- that her first 5 hours overtime have been listed at time and a quarter

- that the units shown in the total columns are hours and minutes. Therefore 2.30 = 2 hours and 30 minutes.
- that the totals for all her time are added up in the final right-hand column and this column is used to work out her pay.

TEST YOURSELF

Peter Fellows works for the same company, in the same section, also at a basic rate of £5 an hour. The same conditions regarding overtime rates and lost time apply for him as did for Janice Thompson. From the information given on his clock card below, calculate his gross pay for the week.

WORKS NO 329	NAME PETER J FELLOWS WEEK ENDING 5 MARCH 19—						STANDARD WEEK HRS 37½	
	MON	TUES	WED	THUR	FRI	SAT	SUN	
IN	0800	0802	0800	0758	0800	0800	0900	
OUT	1200	1200	1200	1200	1200	1100	1200	
IN	1300	1300	1300	1300	1300			
OUT	1630	1730	1630	1630	1630			
IN	1700			1700				
OUT	1900			2000				TOTALS
LOST TIME								
TOTAL ORD								
TOTAL 1¼								
TOTAL 1½								
TOTAL 2								

	No of Hrs	Rate	Earnings
Ord Time	....	....	....
Time + 1¼	....	....	....
Time + 1½	....	....	....
Double Time	....	....	....
		GROSS PAY £	....

Time sheets

Like clock cards, time sheets are used to record the number of hours an employee spends at work. The difference is that time sheets are used for those employees who do not spend all their working hours on one site, eg:

- builders, joiners, electricians working for a building contractor on a housing development. The time sheets would have to be counter-signed by the foreman before submission to the office
- 'temps' working for employment agencies who are working for different organisations during different weeks. The time sheet would have to be validated by the employing organisation before submission to the agency
- a design engineer who divides his time between different projects each day. The time sheet would be used to cost each particular job.

DEDUCTIONS

Unfortunately for employees, various deductions are made from their gross pay by the organisation. The pay they actually take home is their **net pay** – pay after deductions.

There are two types of deductions:

- **statutory** deductions (those required by law)
- **voluntary** deductions (those agreed to or requested by the employee).

Statutory deductions

The main statutory deductions are

- income tax and
- National Insurance.

Both are collected by organisations using the **PAYE** system (Pay As You Earn) and are calculated in relation to the amount earned by each employee in a **fiscal year** (from 6 April one year to 5 April the next).

Voluntary deductions

These can include:

- trade union subscriptions
- charity donations
- social club subscriptions.

In all these cases the employee has a choice – whether to pay or not. However, in some cases, eg charity payments, the amount paid may be tax deductible up to a specified amount each year.

Pension contributions

Contributions towards a pension fall somewhere between statutory and voluntary deductions.

The government offers its own pension scheme (called **SERPS**) and employees who contribute towards this scheme pay a *higher* rate of National Insurance.) This is known as **not contracting out**.

As an alternative an employee can have his or her *own* private pension scheme or contribute towards the company pension scheme instead of paying towards SERPS. The employee pays a *lower* rate of National Insurance and this is known as **contracting out**.

SPECIAL NOTE

An employee is not allowed, by law, to contract out of SERPS *without* joining a private or company scheme. An alternative word used for some pensions is **Superannuation**.

Calculating income tax payable

- Each year many people receive a Tax Return. They must complete and send it to their Inland Revenue office. On this return they state their total income, allowable expenses, dependents (eg children) etc.
- The Inland Revenue uses this information to calculate the

taxable income. This is obtained by taking into account how much each person earns and receives each year and setting against their income certain **allowances**. Allowances may include:

- personal allowance
- married couple's allowance – when added to the personal allowance it gives the same allowance in total as the previous married man's allowance
- mortgage interest
- certain expenses incurred during employment but not reimbursed by the employer
- pension contributions.

- From these figures the Inland Revenue calculate the amount of **free pay** each individual can earn – that is the amount they are allowed to earn before paying tax.

- The Inland Revenue notifies the individual of his tax free pay and gives him a **code number** by sending him a **Notice of Coding**. They notify his employer by sending him form **P9**.

- The Wages Department uses the code number to look up the amount of free pay for the employee each week or month by referring to **Tax Tables** issued by the Inland Revenue. The amount of free pay to that date is shown opposite each code number in **Table A** of the tax tables.

- The *difference* between the free pay and the total gross pay is **taxable pay**. The Wages Clerk then refers to **Table B** of the Tax Tables. This gives the tax due on taxable pay to date, up to certain weekly or monthly limits. (Tables C and D cover employees who earn more than these limits.)

- The wages clerk records the information on a **Tax Deduction Card** (Form **P11**) for each employee.

- If an employee changes jobs during the year the wages clerk has to prepare a **P45**, giving details of the employee's **code number**, total pay to date, tax due and tax paid to date. This again is in three parts:

  - Part 1 is sent to the Inland Revenue immediately so they know that person is no longer employed by his old company.

- Parts 2 and 3 are taken by the employee to his or her new job. Part 2 is sent to the Inland Revenue to inform them where that person is now working.
- Part 3 is handed to the Wages Department of the new company so that they can continue to deduct income tax at the correct rate.

- If no P45 is given to a new employer then the Wages Department at that company will send to the Inland Revenue for form **P46**. This means that the new employee will be taxed on an **emergency coding**, currently **300L**, (and pay more income tax) until everything is sorted out. On an emergency code, the employee's tax is *always* calculated on a Week 1 or Month 1 basis.

Because this means the employee is taxed at a high rate, the Wages Department will give the new employee a form **P15** – a *coding claim* – which he or she must complete and send to the Inland Revenue as soon as possible so that a tax code can be allocated as soon as possible.

SPECIAL NOTE

This procedure only applies to employees paid more than the PAYE threshold amount (ie the specified amount of pay above which PAYE must be operated).

- Employees paid less than this amount do not require a P11 to be completed each week but the employer should keep a record of the employee's name, address and the amount paid each day.

- Self-employed people do not pay income tax by the PAYE system. Instead their Tax Return is completed from their year end accounts showing their profit and allowable expenses for the year. They are then sent a bill for tax due direct from the Inland Revenue and have to pay this in two six-monthly instalments.

CHECK IT YOURSELF

It is important that you see the tax forms referred to in the last section yourself. The main ones you need to collect are:

- a Tax Return
- a Notice of Coding
- form P11 (see page 99)

- form P60
- form P45.

It is obviously also useful if you can see a copy of a P46 and P15 as well. Ask your tutor for help or, if you are working, the wages section of your organisation will be able to give you some of the forms.

The Inland Revenue also issue many useful booklets for students. Try to get your own copy of

- *Income Tax and School Leavers*
- *How we work out your tax code*
- *Thinking of Taking Someone On? – PAYE for Employers*

REMEMBER – you should know how tax works, not just for your job, but for *yourself!*

TEST YOURSELF
Stage 1

Below are given the weekly wages for four men. It is now week 23 of the tax year. Can you work out how much gross pay each man will have received *by the end of this week* (assuming no overtime or other payments)?

a James Whittaker £210 pw   **c** Ismail Badruddin £195

b Andrew Bryant £185 pw   **d** Simon Edwards £240

Check your answers with your tutor before you carry on.

Stage 2

Following is an extract from Table A – Free Pay for week 23 of the tax year.

TABLE A — FREE PAY

WEEK 23
Sept 7 to Sept 13

Code	Total free pay to date	Code	Total free pay to date	Code	Total free pay to date	Code	Total free pay to date	Code	Total free pay to date	Code	Total free pay to date	Code	Total free pay to date	Code	Total free pay to date
	£		£		£		£		£		£		£		£
0	NIL	61	273.93	121	539 35	181	804 77	241	1069 96	301	1335 38	361	1600 80	421	1866 22
1	8.51	62	278.30	122	543 72	182	809 14	242	1074 56	302	1339 75	362	1605 17	422	1870 59
2	12.88	63	282 67	123	548 09	183	813 51	243	1078 93	303	1344 35	363	1609 77	423	1874 96
3	17 25	64	287 27	124	552 46	184	817 88	244	1083 30	304	1348 72	364	1614 14	424	1879 56
4	21 85	65	291 64	125	557 06	185	822 25	245	1087 67	305	1353 09	365	1618 51	425	1883 93
5	26 22														
6	30 59	66	296.01	126	561 43	186	826 85	246	1092 27	306	1357 46	366	1622 88	426	1888 30
7	34 96	67	300.38	127	565 80	187	831 22	247	1096 64	307	1362 06	367	1627 25	427	1892 67
8	39 56	68	304 75	128	570 17	188	835 59	248	1101 01	308	1366 43	368	1631 85	428	1897 27
9	43 93	69	309.35	129	574 77	189	839 96	249	1105 38	309	1370 80	369	1636 22	429	1901 64
10	48 30	70	313 72	130	579 14	190	844 56	250	1109 75	310	1375 17	370	1640 59	430	1906 01

Write down the total free pay to date for the four men with code numbers:

a James Whittaker 184L   **c** Ismail Badruddin 244L
b Andrew Bryant   304H   **d** Simon Edwards   309H

Again check your answers before you proceed.

Stage 3

If you now *subtract* the free pay you calculated at Stage 2, from the total pay to date you worked out at Stage 1, you can find the *taxable* pay of each employee so far this year. Write down the taxable pay of each man named above.

Stage 4

You can now look up the total tax due by each man so far this year in Table B. Below are extracts from Table B. For each person, if the exact amount is not listed, look up the tax due on the next *smallest* amount. Therefore £500.72 = £500. Now calculate the total tax due to date for each man.

Total TAXABLE PAY to date	Total TAX DUE to date	Total TAXABLE PAY to date	Total TAX DUE to date	Total TAXABLE PAY to date	Total TAX DUE to date	Total TAXABLE PAY to date	Total TAX DUE to date
£	£	£	£	£	£	£	£
2901	725.25	2961	740.25	4006	1001.50	4066	1016.50
2902	725.50	2962	740.50	4007	1001.75	4067	1016.75
2903	725.75	2963	740.75	4008	1002.00	4068	1017.00
2904	726.00	2964	741.00	4009	1002.25	4069	1017.25
2905	726.25	2965	741.25	4010	1002.50	4070	1017.50
2906	726.50	2966	741.50	4011	1002.75	4071	1017.75
2907	726.75	2967	741.75	4012	1003.00	4072	1018.00
2908	727.00	2968	742.00	4013	1003.25	4073	1018.25
2909	727.25	2969	742.25	4014	1003.50	4074	1018.50
2910	727.50	2970	742.50	4015	1003.75	4075	1018.75
3396	849.00	3456	864.00	4081	1020.25	4141	1035.25
3397	849.25	3457	864.25	4082	1020.50	4142	1035.50
3398	849.50	3458	864.50	4083	1020.75	4143	1035.75
3399	849.75	3459	864.75	4084	1021.00	4144	1036.00
3400	850.00	3460	865.00	4085	1021.25	4145	1036.25
3401	850.25	3461	865.25	4086	1021.50	4146	1036.50
3402	850.50	3462	865.50	4087	1021.75	4147	1036.75
3403	850.75	3463	865.75	4088	1022.00	4148	1037.00
3404	851.00	3464	866.00	4089	1022.25	4149	1037.25
3405	851.25	3465	866.25	4090	1022.50	4150	1037.50

Stage 5

Below are given the figures to show how much tax each man had paid to date *last week*. From what you found out at Stage 4 (tax now due), can you work out how much tax each man must pay this week?

a James Whittaker £959.25   **c** Ismail Badruddin £813.25
b Andrew Bryant   £694.75   **d** Simon Edwards   £992.00

Quick review

- Earnings each week x number of weeks this tax year = total pay for the year.
- Code number + Table A = free pay for each particular week.
- Total pay – free pay = taxable pay to date.
- Taxable pay to date + Table B = total tax due to date.
- Total tax due to date this week (or month) – total tax to date last week (or month) = tax due this week (or month).

National Insurance

The percentage deducted for National Insurance depends on whether the employee has, or has not, contracted out of SERPS (the State Earnings Related Pension Scheme) in favour of another pension scheme.

All employees earning over a certain amount pay *some* National Insurance as these contributions pay for a number of cash benefits including:

- unemployment benefit
- statutory sick pay
- statutory maternity pay
- the basic state retirement pension
- industrial disablement benefit
- child benefit
- widow's benefit
- death grant.

When a person reaches 16 he or she is sent a National Insurance number by the DSS (Department of Social Security). Each individual keeps the same number throughout his or her working life.

Contributions are payable by *both* employees and employers and are calculated by referring to the National Insurance tables which give the correct amount to be deducted according to the gross pay.

The deductions for National Insurance are also entered on the P11 together with the tax deductions and a cheque covering the *whole* amount deducted for each employee (for National Insurance and income tax) is sent to the Inland Revenue once a month.

TEST YOURSELF

The following is an extract from *not* contracted out National Insurance tables. From this can you state:

- the employer's monthly contributions for a person earning £209?
- the employee's monthly contributions if he or she earns £205
- the total monthly contributions for someone earning £147?

Earnings on which employee's contributions payable 1a	Total of employee's and employer's contributions payable 1b	Employee's contribution payable lc	Employer's contributions
£	£	£	£
143	22.81	9.90	12.91
144	22.99	9.99	13.00
145	23.17	10.08	13.09
146	23.35	10.17	13.18
147	23.53	10.26	13.27
148	23.71	10.35	13.36
149	23.89	10.44	13.45
150	24.07	10.53	13.54
151	24.25	10.62	13.63
152	24.43	10.71	13.72

Earnings on which employee's contributions payable 1a	Total of employee's and employer's contributions payable 1b	Employee's contribution payable lc	Employer's contributions
£	£	£	£
203	36.57	15.30	21.27
204	36.76	15.39	21.37
205	36.95	15.48	21.47
206	37.15	15.57	21.58
207	37.34	15.66	21.68
208	37.54	15.75	21.79
209	37.73	15.84	21.89
210	37.93	15.93	22.00
211	38.12	16.02	22.10
212	38.32	16.11	22.21

SPECIAL NOTE

There are *two* books which contain National Insurance tables. The first is for Not Contracted Out contributions and contains Table A and B and the second is for Contracted Out contributions and contains Tables D and E. Table C applies to both books. The Table to use depends on the employee's age and other circumstances (full details are given at the top of the tables).

Do make sure you refer to the correct Table in each case. The reverse of the P11 includes a column in which you should write the letter of the NI Table to be used for that employee.

WAGES DEPARTMENT DOCUMENTATION

The Wages Department now prepares:

- the individual deductions working sheet for each employee (P11)
- the individual pay advice
- the payroll
- a coin analysis for the money required to pay cash wages.

The P11

A separate P11 is kept for each employee and the same form is used to record:

- earnings week by week or monthly
- income tax and National Insurance for each week or month
- any Statutory Sick Pay (SSP) or Statutory Maternity Pay (SMP).

The pay advice (or pay slip)

The information from the clock card or time sheet (if applicable) plus the information from the P11 is put together to make up each person's pay advice (see later).

A copy is kept by the company as an individual pay record for each employee.

In addition to giving details of total earnings, total tax and National Insurance so far in that tax year, and the details for that particular week or month, the pay advice also gives the method of payment. This is usually marked as either:

- cash
- cheque
- BACS This stands for Bankers' Automated Clearing System and denotes that the employee is paid by credit transfer direct into his bank account (see page 112).

The payroll

This lists each employee in the organisation and gives the following information:

- employee number
- name and department
- total gross wage
- income tax and National Insurance
- voluntary deductions
- total deductions
- calculation of net pay.

Coin analysis

This may be done for the total amount of cash wages or, in a large organisation by department (see page 111).

From the work you have done already you are now ready to start completing the deductions working sheet – the P11. One is completed for each employee every week, the same form being used throughout the year. An organisation must keep the forms for at least three years after use.

The best way to work through this section is to have a copy of National Insurance tables and Tax Tables to hand to look up the amounts yourself at each stage. We have used the following editions: Tax Tables A – 1982 Issue; Tax Tables B – June 1988 Issue; NI (Not Contracted Out) – 5 October 1989 – 5 April 1990. Even if you haven't a set it is still possible to understand the entries, providing you work through the entries in relation to the comments on each.

Stage 1 – The start of the year

Alistair Stott works for Beaver Electronics. During the first week of the tax year he earns £190. He is not contracted out for National Insurance. His tax code is 203H.

- The National Insurance figures (columns 1a to 1c) are completed by copying them from the NI table for not-contracted out male employees between 16 and 65 (Table A). Note that column 1a is *always* entered as a whole number (rounded down to the smaller figure). If Alistair Stott had earned £190.84 we would still have entered £190.

- PAYE income tax figures are entered in columns 2 to 7
  - column 2 is his pay this week (£190). For this week only it is identical to column 3 – total pay to date.
  - column 4 is completed by looking up his *code number* under week 1 in Table A
  - column 5, his taxable pay, is found by subtracting his free pay (column 4) from column 3.
  - column 6, his tax due, is found by looking up his taxable pay figure (rounded to the smaller figure) in Table B. For this week only this is identical to column 7 – his tax deducted this week.

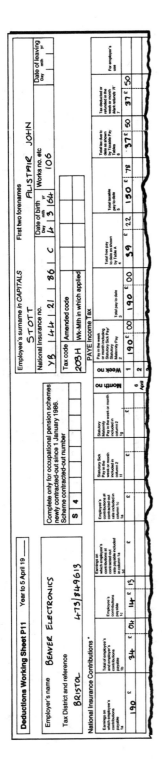

Stage 2 – The second week

This week Alistair Stott earns the same amount. However, in the extract below note how:

- the total pay to date figure (column 3) is now *double* – he has received 2 x £190.
- column 4 is again found by referring to his code number in Table A, but this time under week two.
- column 5 is still calculated by subtracting his free pay in column 4 from column 3.
- his tax due (column 6) is found again by referring to Table B, and this time column 7 is calculated by subtracting the tax he paid the previous week (column 6, line 1) from the total tax now due (column 6, line 2).

National Insurance Contributions *

Earnings on which employee's contributions payable 1a	Total of employee's and employer's contributions payable 1b	Employee's contributions payable 1c	Earnings on which employee's contributions at contracted-out rate payable included in column 1a 1d	Employee's contributions at contracted-out rate included in column 1c 1a	Statutory Sick Pay in the week or month included in column 2 1f	Statutory Maternity Pay in the week or month included in column 2 1g
190	34 04	14 04	13			
190	34 04	14 04	13			

PAYE Income Tax

Month no	Week no	Pay in the week or month including Statutory Sick Pay Statutory Maternity Pay 2	Total pay to date 3	Total free pay to date as shown by Table A 4	Total taxable pay to date 5	Total tax due to date as shown by Taxable Pay Tables 6	Tax deducted or refunded in the week or month Mark refunds 'R' 7	For employer's use
6 April to 5 May 1	1	190 00	190 00	39 22	150 79	37 50	37 50	
	2	190 00	380 00	78 44	301 56	75 25	37 75	
	3							

Stage 3 – a change of earnings

During the next two weeks Alistair Stott earns more than his basic £190 per week. This therefore affects his National Insurance contributions.

- His PAYE income tax entries are also affected. Check out the figures across week 3 and note how his tax deducted for week 3 is the result of his tax due in week 2 (column 6, line 2) being subtracted from his tax now due (column 6, line 3).

- The tax to be deducted is omitted from week 4. How much is it?

PAYE Income Tax

Month no	Week no	Pay in the week or month including Statutory Sick Pay Statutory Maternity Pay 2	Total pay to date 3	Total free pay to date as shown by Table A 4	Total taxable pay to date 5	Total tax due to date as shown by Taxable Pay Tables 6	Tax deducted or refunded in the week or month Mark refunds 'R' 7	For employer's use
6 April to 5 May 1	1	190 00	190 00	39 22	150 79	37 50	37 50	
	2	190 00	380 00	78 44	301 56	75 25	37 75	
	3	215 00	595 00	117 66	477 34	119 25	44 00	
	4	220 00	815 00	156 83	658 12	164 50	44 00	

National Insurance Contributions *

Earnings on which employee's contributions payable 1a	Total of employee's and employer's contributions payable 1b	Employee's contributions payable 1c	Earnings on which employee's contributions at contracted-out rate payable included in column 1a 1d	Employee's contributions at contracted-out rate included in column 1c 1a	Statutory Sick Pay in the week or month included in column 2 1f	Statutory Maternity Pay in the week or month included in column 2 1g
190	34 04	14 04	13			
190	34 04	14 04	13			
215	38 90	16 36				
220	39 87	16 83				

Stage 4 – a change of tax code

In week 5 you are notified by the tax office that Alistair Stott's code number has changed from 203H to 416H. The first thing you must do is cross out his old code number and insert the amended code in the correct box with the week number from which it applies.

If a person's tax code goes *down* they will pay *more* tax. If it goes *up*, they will pay *less* tax. If it goes up quite considerably they may be owed a refund because they have *overpaid* in previous weeks.

This is what has happened with Alistair Stott. If you look up his free pay in Table A (under week 5, remember) for his new code number, you will find his total free pay has increased considerably. You then calculate his total taxable pay in the usual way. When you look up his tax due in Table B and enter the figure you should notice this is *less* than the total tax due the week before. He is therefore owed the *difference* between the two figures, £164.50 – £153.50 = £11. This is marked by an R for refund (often in red).

Deductions Working Sheet P11 Year to 5 April 19 —

Employer's name: BEAVER ELECTRONICS

Tax District and reference: BRISTOL 4-73/84613

Complete only for occupational pension schemes newly contracted-out since 1 January 1986.
Scheme contracted-out number

| S | 4 | | | | | | | |

National Insurance Contributions

Earnings on which employee's contributions payable 1a	Total of employee's and employer's contributions payable 1b	Employee's contributions payable 1c	Earnings on which employee's contributions at contracted-out rate payable included in column 1a 1d	Employee's contributions at contracted-out rate payable included in column 1d 1e	Statutory Sick Pay in the week or month included in column 2 1f	Statutory Maternity Pay in the week or month included in column 2 1g
190	34 04	14 15				
190	34 04	14 13				
215	38 90	16 38				
220	39 81	16 83				
200	35 98	15 03				

Employee's surname in CAPITALS: **STOTT**   First two forenames: **ALISTAIR JOHN**

National Insurance no.: YB 44 21 86 C   Date of birth in figures: 4 13 64   Works no. etc: 106   Date of leaving in figures

Tax code: **203H**   Amended code: **416H**   Wk-Mth in which applied: **5**

Month no 3	Week no	Pay in the week or month including Statutory Sick Pay/Statutory Maternity Pay 2	Total pay to date	Total free pay to date as shown by Table A 4	Total taxable pay to date 5	Total tax due to date as shown by Taxable Pay Tables 6	Tax deducted or refunded in the week or month Mark refunds 'R' 7	For employee's use
6 April to 5 May 1	1	190 00	190 00	39 00	160	22	37	37 50	
	2	190 00	380 00	78 00	301	44	75	25 75	
	3	215 00	595 00	117 00	477	80	119	28 44	
	4	220 00	815 00	156 00	658	81	164	50 45	
6 May to	5	200 00	1015 00	400 00	614	90	153	50 11 00 R

Contracting out

Different National Insurance tables are used for employees who have contracted out of SERPS, depending on whether they are paying at standard or reduced rate. The following extract from a P11 shows the entries for a man aged between 16 and 65, earning the same amount per week as Alistair Stott, but this time using the contracted out tables.

Note that 5 columns are now completed – 1a to 1e – again copied from the tables. In this case Table D, for standard rate, is used.

National Insurance Contributions*

Earnings on which employee's contributions payable 1a	Total of employee's and employer's contributions payable 1b	Employee's contributions payable 1c	Earnings on which employee's contributions at contracted-out rate payable included in column 1a 1d	Employee's contributions at contracted-out rate included in column 1c 1a	Statutory Sick Pay in the week or month included in column 2 1f	Statutory Maternity Pay in the week or month included in column 2 1g	Month no
190 £	25 £ 48	11 £ 18	147 £	10 £ 32	£	£	
190	25 48	11 18	147	10 32			6 April to 5 May 1
215	28 89	12 93	172	12 07			
220	29 67	13 28	177	12 42			
200	26 84	11 88	157	11 02			6 May to 5 June

CHECK IT YOURSELF

- Can you remember why someone might contract out of SERPS?
- Why do they still have to pay something towards National Insurance?
- Why might the tax code of an individual change during the year? Discuss this with your tutor if you are not sure.
- Discuss with your tutor the ways in which the government, in its March Budget, can affect the amount of tax and National Insurance people pay.

For these exercises you need blank P11 forms, National Insurance and Tax Tables.

- Karen Smythe is employed by Beaver Electronics on a basic weekly wage of £115 per week. Her tax code is 125L and her National Insurance number is YB 44 88 01 D. Her date of birth is 12 October 1971 and her works number is 482. She has contracted out for National Insurance (scheme number S48927381) and she pays at the standard rate. Calculate Karen's tax up to and including week 4 of the tax year.
- Roger Lomax is also employed by Beaver Electronics. His basic wage is £175 per week, his tax code is 120H and his National Insurance number is YD 73 92 84 D. His date of birth is 14 February 1962 and his works number is 301. Roger has not contracted out for National Insurance.
  - Calculate his tax up to and including week 3 of the tax year.
  - During weeks 4 and 5 he works overtime. His gross pay in week 4 is £217 and in week 5 £220.50. Calculate his tax for these 2 weeks.
  - In week 6 you receive notification from the tax office that his code number has changed to 384H. Assuming he earns his basic wage that week, calculate any tax or refund due.
  - Continue to calculate his tax for weeks 7 and 8.

 PUTTING IT ALL TOGETHER – MAKING OUT THE PAYSLIP

The information from the clock card and the P11 is now put together to make out the **payslip**. The way this is done is shown on the next page for week 31 of the tax year.

The only additional information you need to know is that Joseph Heys works in Production (coded as department 5) and that he pays £1.25 per week in union dues. He has also opted to be paid in cash.

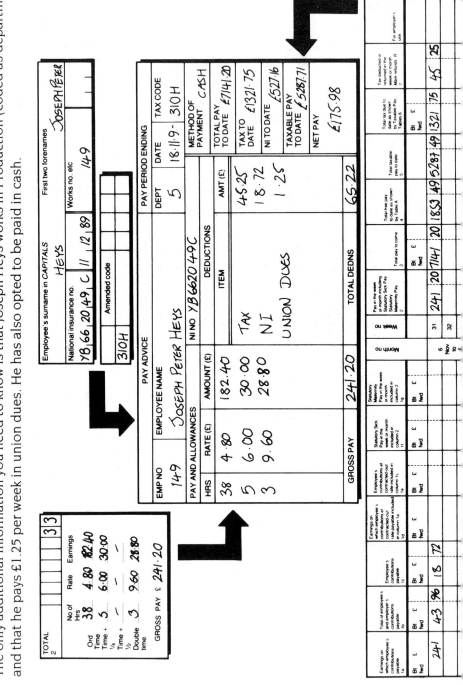

TEST YOURSELF

Christopher Doughty works for Beaver Electronics in the maintenance section (department 7). He works a basic 37½ hour week and is paid £5.40 an hour. His works number is 101 and his National Insurance number is YC 66 02 93 B.

- During the first week of the tax year he works
  - 37½ hours at basic rate
  - 6 hours at time and a quarter
  - 4 hours at time and a half.
  Calculate his gross wage for the week.

- Christopher Doughty's tax code is 400H and he has not contracted out for National Insurance. His date of birth is 14 May 1954. From this information complete his P11 for the week.

- Make out his pay advice for the week. Note that he pays union dues of £1.00 per week, and also contributes £1.00 a week to charity. He is paid by credit transfer.

OTHER STATUTORY PAYMENTS AND DEDUCTIONS

Month end procedures

Within 14 days of the end of a tax month the employer must complete a **P30 BC(Z)** payslip for the Collector of Taxes. This shows the total of all PAYE and National Insurance contributions the organisation has collected during that tax month *less* any tax refunds, SSP or SMP payments and SSP or SMP compensation amounts. The completed payslip is then sent to the Accounts Office of the Inland Revenue with the amount payable.

Year end procedures

At the end of each fiscal year the employer must complete an **end of year return** (Form **P14**) for each employee. This is in three copies:

- top copy for the DSS
- second copy for the Inland Revenue
- third copy for the employee (Form P60).

The P14 gives details of all pay received, tax deductions, NI contributions and SSP or SMP payments during the last tax year. The organisation batches all its top and second copies together, and sends *both* batches to the Inland Revenue (who forwards the DSS their set) with form **P35** – the Employer's Annual Statement, Declaration and Certificate.

In addition the employer must give information about expenses and benefits paid to certain employees during the year on form **P11D**. Further details on form P11D are given in the chapter on Processing Documents Relating to Goods and Services in the section on expense claims.

 SPECIAL NOTE
- The details given above for year end procedures relate to *manual* payroll procedures. Organisations operating a computerised payroll can, with prior permission, send their end of year returns on magnetic tape or floppy disk to the DSS at Newcastle who will provide both the Inland Revenue and the employer with a data listing.
- *All* PAYE records and documents must be kept for at least 3 years after the end of the tax year to which they relate.

 ## OTHER STATUTORY PAYMENTS AND DEDUCTIONS

Statutory Sick Pay (SSP)
Employees who are ill for more than three consecutive days must complete a **self-certification form (SC1)** which they can get from their employer or their doctor. After six days, sickness must be covered by a doctor's note.

The first three days are known as **waiting days**. After this time, up to a maximum of 28 weeks in any one tax year, an employer is responsible for paying the employee SSP. After 28 weeks the employee has to claim **invalidity benefit**.

Not all employees qualify for SSP, for example those whose earnings are below the level at which NI contributions must be paid. It is important to check, in each case, if an employee is eligible for SSP.

Days for which SSP can be paid are referred to as **qualifying days** and the period when an employee is sick (including Saturdays and Sundays) is referred to as a **PIW – Period of Incapacity for Work**. If the gap between PIWs is less than 8 weeks the PIWs *link* and SSP can be paid from the first day of sickness as waiting days are served only once in any PIW. Possible links are checked using SSP Tables.

To calculate SSP the employee's earnings are first calculated on an *average* basis, eg for a weekly paid employee the average weekly wage is the gross pay for the last 8 pay days divided by 8. The earnings figure determines whether the employee receives SSP at standard or lower rate. The amount payable is calculated on a *daily* basis, using SSP Table A (standard rate) or Table B (lower rate).

Many employers supplement the minimum amounts paid under SSP with their own Occupational Sick Pay scheme but this is voluntary, and the organisation can only reclaim the SSP amount paid.

SSP is treated as earnings and included in the gross pay of an individual. Form **SSP2** is available on which employers can record all their SSP payments if they wish. The organisation can recover the gross amount of SSP paid *plus* an additional amount of compensation (currently 7% of the total gross SSP). In addition all gross SSP payments must be included on the end of year return (P14) and P35.

Statutory Maternity Pay (SMP)

Women can apply for SMP provided they have been employed with the company for at least 6 months by the end of the 26th week of pregnancy and have earned enough, in the last 8 weeks, to pay NI contributions. There are two rates of SMP, lower and higher rate. Long-serving employees are usually eligible for the higher rate, which is paid only for the first 6 weeks.

A woman claiming SMP must present a maternity certificate to her employer which gives her expected week of confinement (ie the week the baby is due to be born). This information is then checked against the SMP tables to give the **qualifying week** – ie the week when she must have been working to qualify for SMP. The tables also show the first week for which SMP can be paid. This is not a fixed week, as some women prefer to work nearer to the birth than others *but*:

- SMP cannot be paid for any week in which the woman earns her normal wage
- the maximum time limit for SMP is always 18 weeks.

The lower rate is a fixed weekly payment, given in the front of the SMP tables. At present the higher rate SMP is 90% of the *average* of the employee's wage (eg for weekly paid employees this is calculated as for SSP – the last 8 pay days divided by 8). Again, employers may supplement the state payment with their own Occupational Maternity Pay scheme but, as for SSP, only the SMP amount, plus a 7% compensation payment, can be deducted from the end of month amount due to the Collector of Taxes.

SPECIAL NOTE

When completing a P11 for an employee paid SSP or SMP you must remember that these payments are *taxable*. Therefore:

- columns 1b, 1c and 1e must show the NI contributions due on the total payment including SSP or SMP
- SSP or SMP must be shown as a separate figure in columns 1f or 1g
- the SSP or SMP amount must be included in the taxable pay figure in column 2.

CHECK IT YOURSELF

- Obtain a copy of form SC1 (Self-Certification form) and practise completing it with your tutor.
- If you are working, find out the arrangements for SSP and SMP in your particular organisation. Does your company have an Occupational Sick Pay or Maternity Pay scheme? If so, does this apply to all employees?
- The facts given above on SSP and SMP apply to England, Scotland and Wales but there are some differences you should note if you work in Northern Ireland. If this applies to you, discuss any variations with your tutor.

Attachment of earnings

This is a deduction from wages which occurs when a Court of Law orders that a certain amount must be deducted from an individual's wage or salary each pay day, eg:

- to pay an unpaid debt
- to pay maintenance payments which had not been paid to a family in accordance with an original Court Order.

When making the order to pay, the Court takes into account the amount the person needs to live on each week. The Court then issues the order to the employer, subject to a **Protected Earnings Rate**. This is the net amount of pay the employee must earn *before* the Attachment of Earnings order can be applied eg

> Attachment of earnings amount = £20
> Protected Earnings Rate = £100
>
> Net pay – week 1 = £150 therefore £20 payable
> Net pay – week 2 = £100 therefore nothing payable
> Net pay – week 3 = £110 therefore £10 payable
> Net pay – week 4 = £170 therefore £20 payable

Remember that this is a deduction which occurs after net pay has been calculated. It therefore appears only on the pay slip – not on the P11.

It is important to note that the deductions are calculated from week to week, ie arrears are not payable if an employee earns more money one week (See week 4.) However, anyone "managing" their earnings so as to minimise Attachment of Earnings could be the subject of a court investigation.

OTHER PAYMENTS, ALLOWANCES AND DEDUCTIONS

The other obvious payment is holiday pay – each individual working for an organisation is entitled to a stated number of days holiday each year in addition to statutory days (eg Christmas Day). This will be clearly set out in the **contract of employment**.

Taxable allowances paid to employees can include:

- bonus payments and commission
- additional responsibility allowance
- stand-by allowance
- payment for weekend duty or unsocial hours.

Non-taxable allowances can include:

- travelling expenses
- car allowance
- uniform
- laundry.

Deductions can include:

- overpayments in previous periods
- contribution to benevolent fund
- contribution to widow's fund
- SAYE (Save as You Earn).

CHECK IT YOURSELF

For each of the allowances and deductions above, discuss with your tutor the type of occupations when such payments or deductions would be made.

SPECIAL NOTE

In this chapter you have practised undertaking wage and salary calculations in relation to clock cards and other information based on the same week as the wage was paid. In reality, this does not always occur as virtually all organisations pay wages and salaries **in arrears**.

- monthly staff are often paid during the last week of the month, they are therefore paid four weeks in arrears.
- hourly paid and weekly paid staff usually work a week **in hand**. They are therefore paid on a Friday for the work they did the previous week.

This system is necessary to give wages staff time to complete all the documentation, check on which days SSP should be paid etc.

The important fact to remember is that you should always refer to Tax and NI Tables for the week in which payment is being made *regardless* of when the work was carried out.

WAGES PAYMENT SYSTEMS

When employees start working for an organisation they have the choice of being paid in cash, by cheque or by credit transfer. If they choose credit transfer then their wages or salary will be paid direct into their bank account each week or month.

If you work in a large wages department then you may be involved in all three methods of payment.

Cash payments

If wages are being paid in cash then the coinage must be such as to enable the wages clerk to put the right coins in each wage packet, without an excess of small coins!

This is worked out by undertaking a **coin analysis** as shown on the example below. In this case there is a small company who pays four employees in cash weekly.

Employee 001	£178.16
Employee 002	£201.56
Employee 003	£120.14
Employee 004	£164.85

The amounts shown are the **net** wages (ie after all deductions have been made). This is the actual amount each employee will receive.

This is now worked out in terms of the notes and coins required to make up each amount and the totals are then cross-checked.

Total	£50	£20	£10	£5	£1	50p	20p	10p	5p	2p	1p
£178.16	2	3	1	1	3			1	1		1
£201.56	3	1	2	2	1	1			1		1
£120.14	2		1	1	5			1		2	
£164.85	2	2	1	2	4	1	1	1	1		
	9	6	5	6	13	2	1	3	3	2	2
£664.71	£450	£120	£50	£30	£13	£1	20p	30p	15p	4p	2p

> ### ! SPECIAL NOTE
> Wages are never made up with just large denomination notes. The employee may want to catch the bus home! For that reason, note how the employee who earns £120.14 is *not* just given 2 × £50 notes, 1 × £20 note and 14p in change!

> ### ✓ TEST YOURSELF
> Work out a coin analysis for four employees paid £152.19, £180.62, £78.20 and £129.46. Do not pay anyone more than *two* £50 notes.

🔑 *Cheque payments*

Some employees prefer to be paid by cheque. Cheques are made out in the Wages Section and then they must be signed – usually two signatures are required. Companies who pay out a large number of cheques may have an automatic cheque signing machine which is obviously kept locked when not in use.

🔑 *Credit transfer (BACS)*

This is becoming an ever more popular method of being paid.

- *employers* prefer it because
  - handling less cash means there are fewer security problems
  - the banks undertake a considerable amount of the administrative work
  - very large companies which process wages by computer can take their computer tapes to the bank for onward processing

- fewer pay packets to make up may mean fewer wages staff are required for routine jobs
- there are no queues outside the wages office every Friday.

- *employees* prefer it because
  - they are less likely to lose any money or have any money stolen because they will not be carrying around large amounts.
  - they are less tempted to spend too much on pay day because they feel 'well off'
  - it is simpler and more convenient
  - if they are ill or on holiday they know that any money due does not need collecting.

The credit transfer system

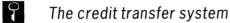

Computerisation has revolutionised the automatic credit transfer systems offered by the banks for wages. Although the services can differ slightly, depending on the bank and whether the company is paying wages locally or nationally, the same type of procedure is usually followed. Transfer payments to employees working abroad are not undertaken by the usual credit transfer system but can be made via Standard Transfer or Urgent Transfer payment systems. Details of these methods of payment are given in the chapter on Processing Payments.

1 Employees who wish to be paid by Credit Transfer complete a special form giving information on:
   - the name of their bank or building society
   - the branch address and sort code
   - the name of their bank account (eg a married couple may have a joint account showing both their names)
   - the account number.
2 The company completes a bank form giving the name of all its employees to be paid by this method and the other information detailed on the credit transfer application form. This form is then sent to the bank.
3 The bank puts the information into their computer and allocates a pay reference number to each employee.
4 Three days before the wages are due to be paid the organisation draws up a list of wages or salaries due against each pay reference number and records this information on a

bank schedule. The schedule must be signed by someone in authority.

5   If the schedule is taken to the bank where the company's account is held then the bank automatically deducts the total of the wages from the company's account. If the schedule is taken to another branch then a company cheque must be attached for the total wage bill.

6   The wages are then automatically transferred to each employee's own bank account on pay day.

 SPECIAL NOTE

An organisation which uses a computer to calculate their wages may just send a printout of their wages bill for that week or month to the bank.

Variations

Some banks issue a full printout for companies every week with all the information completed except the amount of the wage to be paid. The wages clerk then:

● completes the amount columns

● crosses through the names of any employees who leave the company

● attaches application forms for any additional or new employees who wish to be paid by credit transfer.

Below is shown an example of the headings on such a form

Branch ref (sort code)	Bank Account No	Previous week's pay	Bank Account Name	Payee No*	Amount

* This is allocated by the bank.

 TEST YOURSELF

You work for John Arkwright and Co Ltd in the Wages Department. Design a simple form which could be given to all employees who wish to be paid by **credit transfer** to obtain all the information you need for the bank.

WAGES AND SECURITY

Paying out large amounts of money in cash obviously causes security problems for any organisation, which is one of the major reasons why organisations prefer to pay their employees by cheque or, better still, credit transfer.

When cash payments are made, several additional security procedures need to be introduced.

- If very large amounts of cash are being brought into the organisation then a security company (eg Securicor) should be used.
- The wage packets must be made up as quickly as possible after the cash is received.
- In a large organisation different parts of the payroll are usually allocated to different clerks who are given the exact amount to make up into pay packets. This is the best way of guarding against mistakes and is known as the 'exhaust' method.
- Wage packets or envelopes should be used which enable employees to check the contents before opening, to prevent fraud.
- The pay office should be sited as centrally as possible to speed up the paying out process.
- Employees must produce identification when collecting their wages and sign for them as received.
- A clear notice is usually displayed instructing employees to check the contents *immediately* (without opening the packet) against the net pay figure. This, too, should be clearly visible without having to open the packet.
- It is usually safer to have two members of staff paying out the wages together, in case of any disputes.
- A proper system must be set up to deal with any uncollected pay packets. They are usually listed and returned to the cashier and a receipt is obtained for them.
- The total of uncollected wage packets must, of course, agree with wages marked on the pay-roll as uncollected.
- A senior member of the wages staff must be available to deal with queries and problems, eg regarding deductions, pay rates and so on.

Confidentiality

Apart from a head for figures, the two most important attributes you can have for working in a Wages Department are *tact* and *discretion*.

People's wages and salaries are highly *confidential*. You must not, therefore, discuss a person's earnings with anyone else.
In addition, queries about discrepancies, tax or earnings must be handled sympathetically and tactfully.

- N*ever* expect an employee to discuss a salary or wage query in front of anyone else.
- N*ever* 'call out' information to anyone.
- Do not leave wages documents where they can be read by people calling at the office.
- If an employee tells you about a personal circumstance he/she wants to keep confidential only refer the matter to your supervisor if there is a query, not the rest of the department.

SPECIAL NOTE

For both security and confidentiality reasons it is unlikely that other members of staff will be able to actually call into the wages office, especially on pay day. Any callers will usually have to remain behind a glass window or at a counter.

Emergencies

Every organisation should have laid down procedures for staff to cope with major emergencies in the wages section. Minor ones may still require a cool head!

Examples of emergencies which may occur are:

- The most obvious of all – an armed raid. Payment of virtually all staff by credit transfer reduces the risk *but* it is possible that the raiders do not know this fact.
  Quite simply most organisations usually instruct wages staff to *take no personal risks*. The money is usually insured and it is absolutely futile trying any heroics – and may even be dangerous for your colleagues.

You will be far more helpful if you watch and listen carefully so that you can give a good description to the police later. Even if raiders are masked you can still notice useful facts, eg height, build, clothes, jewellery/type of watch worn, tattoos, accent etc.

- Missing money is also an emergency situation – especially if it means not all the pay packets can be made up. There is usually a straightforward explanation but it may take some finding, and if staff panic it will not help matters at all.
Assist with any enquiries by:
  - thinking carefully over all you have done
  - answering questions you are asked calmly
  - offering any useful information.

- Staff absences on pay day can create a headache if there are very many people to pay out and not enough staff to deal with them efficiently. In this situation you are likely to get more sympathy from people waiting if they know what the problem is. Don't try to rush the job too quickly, or you will make a mistake.

- A problem, rather than emergency, would occur if, say, a member of staff calls to collect his wage but according to your records it has already been paid out. If this occurs check your pay packets carefully – it could just be that someone has signed on the wrong line of the wages book. Otherwise notify your supervisor immediately.

CHECK IT YOURSELF

Your supervisor has been called out of the wages office for 15 minutes. Make notes on how you would handle *each* of the following problems in her absence and discuss your answers with your tutor.

1. An employee's pay packet is short by £5 – he has checked the packet as instructed, ie without opening it.
2. An employee is angry because he has been allocated the wrong tax code and has received far less than he expected.
3. An employee is claiming he worked ten hours overtime last week but has not been paid for this.
4. An employee returns to your office to say he has been *overpaid* by £10.

Technology update

Today most organisations use computers to calculate their wages and salaries. Information from clock cards can be fed through automatically to link with the figures already put into the computer for basic rates so that gross pay (including overtime) can be calculated automatically.

Employee information is also input into the computer and all salary scales for monthly salaried staff.

The computer will automatically calculate all gross wages, deductions, coin analyses for cash wages, the payroll, departmental analysis and a pay advice slip for each employee. (See Computerised Payroll Packages at the end of this chapter.)

The confidentiality of wages is covered by special passwords. Users are given a password for the area they need. A different password is usually required to access higher level (more confidential) information.

SECTION REVIEW

Having completed this section, you should now be able to:

1   Correctly calculate gross pay from clock cards and time sheets.

2   Differentiate between statutory and voluntary deductions.

3   Correctly calculate statutory and voluntary deductions using tax tables and other reference books.

4   List the tax forms used in calculating income tax.

5   Complete tax forms accurately.

6   Explain the benefits obtainable through National Insurance contributions.

7   Explain the terms **SERPS**, **not contracted out** and **contracted out**.

8 Complete pay slips accurately.

9 Explain how a change in tax code will affect tax paid.

10 Explain the terms **SSP**, **SMP** and **attachment of earnings**.

11 Differentiate between taxable and non-taxable allowances and payments.

12 State the benefits of the credit transfer system.

13 Describe the operation of BACS and the forms required.

14 List the security measures to be taken in relation to wages payments.

15 Explain the action which should be taken in an emergency.

16 Explain the relevance of confidentiality to working in a wages department.

REVIEW QUIZ

True or false?

1 Monthly paid staff are always paid 12 times a year.

2 Trade Union subscriptions are a statutory deduction from wages.

3 Clocking another employee in or out is often punishable by instant dismissal.

4 A P60 gives details of all pay received, tax deductions and refunds during the last tax year.

5 A P35 is prepared when an employee changes jobs.

Complete the blanks . . .

6 Employees can choose whether or not to contract out of

....

7 The difference between total gross pay and free pay is called

....

8 BACS on a pay packet means the employee is paid by ....

Work it out

9 Make out a coin analysis for five employees paid as follows:

Employee 001	£134.25
Employee 002	£180.05
Employee 003	£74.50
Employee 004	£111.17
Employee 005	£158.39

Do not pay anyone more than *two* £50 notes.

10 Brian Watkins works in the Production Department of Beaver Electronics (department 5) and is paid £3.80 an hour for a basic 38 hour week. His works number is 202.

- During the first week of the tax year he worked:
  - 38 hours at basic rate
  - 5 hours at time and a quarter
  - 3 hours at time and a half
  - 3 hours at double time.
  Calculate his gross wage for the week.

- His tax code at present is 100H and his date of birth is 7 June 1966. He has not contracted out for National Insurance (number YL 49 00 64 D). From this information complete his P11 for the week.
- Brian pays £1.25 per week in Union dues and £1.00 per week towards the sports and social fund. He is paid in cash. Make out his pay advice for the week.
- The following week Brian only works his basic 38 hour week. You receive notification that his tax code number has changed to 440H. Calculate *both* his P11 and his pay advice for the second week.

11 Your company is about to start using the computerised wages service provided at your local bank. You have issued forms to all employees asking them for information about their accounts and these have been returned to you.

Before you fill in the actual bank form you want to make a draft copy of your list.

Write up headings as shown below:

Branch ref	Account No	Account Name	Amount Paid

a From the information given below complete the branch reference (sort code), account number and bank account name columns, putting the information in *alphabetical* order of employee. Leave the final column blank.

02-39-29	28392787	Mr T E and Mrs L Salida
30-40-93	38270938	Mr Jack Emborsky
30-45-29	83798378	Miss Cathy Bowan-Smith
50-30-87	28279827	Mr Steven McGuire
20-42-38	58473987	Mr Liam Murphy
04-30-40	28798738	Mr K and Mrs A. Chitnis

b The wages for last week have been jotted down against the initials of each employee. Enter these correctly. What was the total wage bill last week?

LM – £204.57
JE – £187.54
AC – £93.24
CB-S – £74.23
TS – £122.10
SM – £142.80

Appendix – Computerised Payroll Packages

Payroll packages are very popular in many companies because they save hours of work calculating and producing wages documentation.

The package itself – whichever one you use – will actually be a very sophisticated form of database. The package will already have been programmed with the latest National Insurance and Income Tax rates. If these change during the year the suppliers of the package send an updated disk to their customers containing the new information. This is then merely loaded into the computer and the old rates are automatically revised.

For this reason organisations which buy a payroll package usually have to register their purchase and are often given a special reference number. This reference number then usually has to be entered into the computer the first time the system is used, before it will work.

Setting up the system

When a payroll package is first purchased a minimum of two types of information must be entered into the system:

1   Details about the **company**, eg.

   - company name
   - number of tax weeks (52 or 53) and number of tax months (12 or 13)
   - date computerised payroll commences
   - tax office reference
   - company bank details
   - company pension scheme details
   - overtime rates
   - weekly and hourly pay rates
   - standard hours for each category of employee
   - other pay (both taxable and non-taxable, eg commission)
   - details of unions and union deductions
   - other deductions

- holiday pay information
- employee pension rates.

2 Details about each **employee**, eg

- full name and title
- employee number
- address
- date of birth
- date joined company
- National Insurance number and category
- tax code
- whether hourly, weekly or monthly paid
- rate of pay (or salary if monthly paid)
- method of payment (eg cash, cheque or credit transfer)
- bank details if paid by credit transfer
- union details
- pension scheme details
- previous pay and tax information (form P11)
- National Insurance information
- statutory sick pay information.

All this information is usually **constant** (unchanging) data. The company details will rarely, if ever, change.

The employee details on such items as pay to date will be updated automatically by the computer. Amendments to a record will only be needed if any employee is promoted, his tax code changes or he moves house, changes his bank etc.

When an employee leaves the company his record will, of course, be deleted once his P45 and other details have been completed. New records must obviously be completed for any new personnel joining the company.

CHECK IT YOURSELF
When a computerised payroll system is first installed it is usual to run both this **and** the manual system simultaneously for the first few weeks.

Variable data

To operate the system, **variable** pay data has to be added for each employee's record each week or month. This is called variable because it changes from one time period to another and includes such information as

- hours worked
- overtime
- additional payments due (eg holiday bonus)
- sick pay due
- deductions due.

This information is entered for *each* employee.

Payroll processing

The system can then be asked automatically to

- calculate the net pay for each employee
- analyse this and print out a report for each department
- print payslips
- print out a coin analysis
- make out a list of cheques required or print the cheques themselves
- print out a list of credit transfers
- print out a complete pay listing for the company.

Year end process

At the end of the financial year the computer will also produce P60s and P35s as required and update the file for the year.

SECTION REVIEW

Having completed this section, you should now be able to:

1   Identify the benefits and disadvantages of operating a computerised payroll package.

2   Differentiate between constant and variable data.

3   Describe the payroll operations which can be carried out by computer.

Maintaining financial records

SPECIAL NOTE

This chapter deliberately goes a little way beyond the exact requirements for the Business Administration (Financial) Award Level 2, in order to:

- give you a good solid foundation for later book-keeping studies
- enable you to see the relevance of double entry book-keeping and the records you must complete to the system as a whole.

The chapter is divided into five sections:

Section 1 – Introduction to Book-Keeping and Balance Sheets
Section 2 – Double-Entry Book-Keeping
Section 3 – Books of Account – Ledgers, Day Books, the Cash Book and the Journal
Section 4 – Final Accounts
Section 5 – VAT Returns and VAT Accounts.

Leaving out Section 4 will not stop you from obtaining accreditation for this unit but will mean that you cannot see the 'end result' of your earlier work.

Section 1 – Introduction to book-keeping and balance sheets

WHAT IS BOOK-KEEPING?

All organisations which handle money record all their financial transactions – the amount they spend on goods and the amount they receive for these, expenses such as wages, maintenance, equipment, heating, money owing to the business, what is owing to suppliers and so on.

This is essential for various reasons:

- The financial records enable the organisation to calculate their profit (or loss) at the end of the year. This information is also required by the tax authorities.
- The organisation can calculate the money that they owe to the Customs and Excise in VAT each quarter. A small company which is not registered for VAT can keep an eye on its **turnover** (the total amount of its sales) to see if it becomes liable to register for VAT.

- If the organisation wants to borrow money from a bank it will have to produce the accounts to prove the business is operating satisfactorily.
- The management will need to keep an eye on all transactions so that they can make sure their decisions are in the best interests of the organisation.

Recording this information in the various accounts books is called **book-keeping**. In a very small company the owner may do his or her own books, perhaps only once or twice a week. In a medium or large organisation it will be done on a daily basis. The book-keeping procedures will be carried out in the Accounts Department and all the financial records may be held – and calculated – on computer.

Accounts terms 1
Throughout this section you will meet various accounts terms. In each case discuss the definition with your tutor if you have any difficulty understanding it.

You have already met the first term above.

Turnover – the total amount of sales made in a year

Capital – the money the owner of the business puts into the company

Assets – the possessions of the company

Liabilities – debts owed by the company (for assets provided by someone else).

WHAT IS A BALANCE SHEET?
A **balance sheet** shows the financial state of a company on a *particular day*. This information is presented in two columns. Usually the left-hand column shows the company's capital and liabilities and the right-hand column shows its assets. These two columns must always *balance*, ie they must be equal.

Formula for accounting
You should try to remember this important equation:

Capital + Liabilities = Assets

PREPARING BALANCE SHEETS

Stage 1

In this section we are going to follow the progress of Alan Brown, a sole trader, who has just started his business. He has provided £6000 himself (his **capital**) and borrowed £4000 from the bank. This is a **liability** because eventually he will have to pay the money back.

At the moment all the money is in his bank account (an **asset**). His first **balance sheet** will look like this:

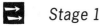

```
                    Balance Sheet of A Brown
                       as at 28 February 19__

    Capital and liabilities    £        Assets              £
    Capital                   6000      Cash at Bank       10000
    Bank Loan                 4000
                              ─────                        ─────
                             10000                         10000
                             ═════                         ═════
    CAPITAL + LIABILITIES    10000    = ASSETS             10000
```

SPECIAL NOTE

- No matter how many transactions Alan Brown carries out, both sides of his balance sheet must *always* be equal – they *must* balance.
- To keep it in balance, every time one thing alters it *must* affect something else. Therefore each transaction = *two* changes.

Stage 2

Balance sheets are normally produced only once a year. However, we are going to follow Alan Brown's progress, via his balance sheet, over the next few days as he sets up his business.

The first thing Alan Brown does is to acquire some premises.
These cost him £3000 and he pays by cheque.

Remember – this must change *two* items. In this case he *gains*
premises but his bank account goes *down* by the same amount.

His balance sheet now looks like this:

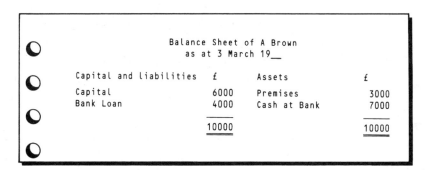

Balance Sheet of A Brown
as at 3 March 19__

Capital and liabilities	£	Assets	£
Capital	6000	Premises	3000
Bank Loan	4000	Cash at Bank	7000
	10000		10000

SPECIAL NOTE

- Because the transaction has affected two items the balance sheet still balances.
- Have you noticed how capital and liabilities are on the left of the page and assets are on the right? Today, some organisations produce their balance sheets like this, others produce them vertically – with the assets first and the liabilities underneath.

Accounts terms 2

Debtor – a person who owes money

Creditor – a person to whom the company owes money.

A debtor is an **asset** because the company will receive money from them.
A creditor is a **liability** because eventually the company must pay its debts.

SPECIAL NOTE

You should have noticed that Alan Brown is in debt to the bank. Therefore technically the bank is a creditor.

If the money borrowed had to be paid back quickly we would have listed the bank as one of our creditors. However, on a balance sheet we put long-term loans (money borrowed which hasn't to be paid back for over a year) separately. We will assume Alan Brown has to pay the money back within the next four years. Therefore it is correct to list the loan on its own.

 ## Stage 3

Alan Brown now decides he must buy some stock.

- He buys £800 of stock in **cash**. This *reduces* his money at the bank but *increases* his stock. Stock is an **asset** because it is something we possess.
- He buys a further £1500 of stock on **credit**. This also increases his stock but it also means he now has the **liability** of a **creditor** to whom he owes money.

```
         Balance Sheet of A Brown
            as at 5 March 19__

Capital and liabilities   £       Assets              £

Capital                  6000     Premises           3000
Bank Loan                4000     Stock              2300
Creditors                1500     Cash at Bank       6200

                        ─────                        ─────
                        11500                        11500
                        ─────                        ─────
```

 ## Stage 4

Alan Brown has one more thing to do before he opens for business. He needs to buy some furniture and fittings for his shop. He then opens the door to his customers.

- His furniture and fittings (called fixtures and fittings on a balance sheet) have cost him £1200 and he paid by cheque.
- On the first day he sells £500 of stock. He puts £200 in the bank and keeps £300 on the premises as cash in hand.
- On the second day he sells £400 of stock on credit to a customer. This customer is now one of Alan Brown's debtors – someone who owes *him* money.

SPECIAL NOTE

Normally, of course, Alan Brown would hope to sell the stock for more than he paid for it – so that he can make a profit. However, at this stage making a profit would complicate things for us! We are therefore going to assume that poor Alan Brown only receives what he paid for his stock and does not make a profit.

His stock therefore decreases by exactly the same value as the money he receives for it.

CHECK IT YOURSELF
- From the balance sheet as it was at Stage 3, and bearing in mind that fixtures and fittings are *assets* (something possessed) try to work out his new balance sheet yourself.
- Work through each transaction carefully with your tutor if you are having difficulty.
- You will find the answer just before the Review Quiz on page 137.

Accounts terms 3

Fixed assets – are those assets which last a long time, eg office furniture and equipment. They are *not* bought to be resold,

Current assets – are those which have a short life – normally because they are meant to be resold or represent cash, eg stock.

CHECK IT YOURSELF
Which of Alan Brown's assets are fixed assets and which are current assets?

SPECIAL NOTE

The assets on a balance sheet are usually subdivided into fixed and current assets. The fixed assets are usually listed first.

```
                    Balance Sheet of A Brown
                        as at 8 March 19__

     Capital and
     liabilities          £       Assets           £         £

     Capital            6000      Fixed assets
     Bank Loan          4000        Premises        3000
     Creditors          1500        Furniture and
                                    fittings        1200
                                                    ────    4200

                                  Current assets

                                  Stock            1400
                                  Debtors           400
                                  Cash at Bank     5200
                                  Cash in Hand      300
                                                   ────    7300

                        ─────                            ─────
                        11500                            11500
                        ═════                            ═════
```

Accounts terms 4

Long term liabilities — debts owed by Alan Brown which he does not have to pay back for over a year (eg his bank loan).

Current liabilities — debts which have to be paid back within the next year – or sooner.

Liquidity — the ease with which an asset can be turned into cash. Obviously cash itself is the most liquid – it already *is* cash!

SPECIAL NOTE

Look down the current assets on the balance sheet. Note that they are listed so that the *most* liquid is at the bottom, the next liquid is the next one up and so on. By the time you get to the top of the balance sheet (the fixed assets) it would be impossible to turn the items into cash without closing the business!

The order on the liabilities side is similar. At the bottom are the debts which must be paid quickly. By the time we reach the top of the balance sheet Alan Brown would have to withdraw his capital and close the business.

Stage 5

On the 11 March Alan Brown buys a motor vehicle, on credit, for £8000. He pays a deposit of £2000 in cash and agrees to pay the remaining £6000 within the next 3 years.

He also pays half of the money he owes to his creditor – £750.

TEST YOURSELF

1   Can you draw up his new balance sheet before you look at the answer?

2   Work out *where* in the order of liabilities you will put his Motor Vehicle Loan, and where, in the order of assets, you will put the vehicle itself.

You will find the answer just before the next Review Quiz.

TEST YOURSELF

Continue to work out Alan Brown's balance sheet for each of the dates below. Obviously if you get one wrong the rest will also be wrong. Therefore check each balance sheet you do with your tutor before moving on to the next date.

14 March   –   Alan Brown is paid £200 by his debtors. He banks the cheque. He buys a further £500 of stock and pays by cheque.

18 March   –   Alan Brown sells £300 of his stock on credit. He inherits £3000 which he puts in the bank. This, of course, increases his capital.

23 March   –   He pays his existing creditors £500 by cheque and buys £1000 of stock and again pays by cheque.

26 March   –   Alan Brown sells £800 of stock for cash. His debtors pay him £150 which he keeps on the premises. He buys a further £300 of stock on credit. He buys additional furniture for £200 and pays by cheque.

Accounts terms 5

Gross profit   –   the difference between the cost price of stock and the selling price

Net profit	–	what is left out of the gross profit after all the expenses have been deducted, eg heating, rent etc
Drawings	–	the money the owner takes out of the business for his own private use
Trading account	–	the account where **gross** profit is calculated
Profit and loss account	–	the account where **net** profit is calculated.

TEST YOURSELF

Can you remember the first formula for a balance sheet?

Capital + Liabilities = Assets

If Alan Brown buys stock for £3000 and sells it for £5000, then although his stock will decrease his bank account will increase *but not by the same amount*.

What will then happen to the balance sheet?

PROFIT AND THE BALANCE SHEET

If we just alter the two entries for stock and cash at the bank, the balance sheet will no longer balance, because Alan Brown's assets have increased by £2000. To compensate for this we have to put his **profit** *on the other side*. Our formula now becomes:

Capital + Profit + Liabilities = Assets

which becomes

New capital + Liabilities = Assets

SPECIAL NOTE

- Whereas profit will *increase* capital, losses will *decrease* capital.
- In real life Alan Brown would have had some expenses involved with making his profit which, for now, we are going to ignore. However, it should be noted that it is always the *net profit* figure which is included in the balance sheet – the profit once the expenses have been deducted.

DRAWINGS AND THE BALANCE SHEET

Alan Brown needs to live, and to do this he will draw money out of his business. He will probably do this by taking money out of the bank.

Because this will *reduce* his assets, the balance sheet will not balance unless we make a compensatory entry on the other side.

Therefore our formula now becomes:

Capital + Liabilities − Drawings = Assets

Stage 6

Let's rejoin Alan Brown at the end of February one year later. He has now been in business twelve months, has made a profit and withdrawn some money to live on.

His balance sheet looks like this:

```
                    Balance Sheet of A Brown
                      as at 28 February 19__
Capital and Liabilities  £        £      Assets                    £       £

Capital balance          9000            Fixed assets
Add net profit           7600
                         ____            Premises                  3000
                        16600            Fixtures and fittings     2000
Less drawings            5600            Motor vehicles            8000
                                11000                             ____    13000

Long-term liabilities                    Current assets

                                         Stock                     2300
Bank loan                3000            Debtors                    800
Motor vehicle loan       4000            Cash at Bank              2600
                         ____    7000    Cash in Hand               500
Current liabilities                                               ____     6200
  Creditors              1200
                                19200                                     19200
```

CHECK IT YOURSELF

- Compare this balance sheet with the last one you produced for him. What has Alan Brown been doing this year besides making a profit?
- After one year of use do you think his motor vehicle would still be worth the same as he paid for it? Discuss what would really have happened with your tutor. What is this called?
- The total amount of money involved in a business is called the **capital employed**. The capital employed in Alan Brown's business is now £19200. What was it when he first started?
  - Work out how much it has increased.
  - Look back over his activities with your tutor. Can you identify what activities increased it through the year?

SECTION REVIEW

Having completed this section, you should now be able to:

1 State why organisations record financial transactions.

2 Identify the main components of a balance sheet.

3 Explain how a balance sheet will change to show the financial state of a company on a particular day.

4 Define the terms **turnover**, **capital**, **liquidity** and **drawings**.

5 Differentiate between each of the following
  - assets and liabilities
  - debtors and creditors
  - fixed and current assets
  - long term and current liabilities
  - gross and net profit.

6 Draw up a balance sheet with assets and liabilities shown in the correct order.

7 Define the term **capital employed** and explain the activities which will cause this to increase or decrease.

Here are the answers to the balance sheet exercises on pages 131 and 133.

```
                    Balance Sheet of A Brown
                       as at 8 March 19__

    Capital and liabilities   £       Assets                    £

    Capital                 6000    Premises              3000
    Bank Loan               4000    Fixtures and fittings 1200
    Creditors               1500    Stock                 1400
                                    Debtors                400
                                    Cash at Bank          5200
                                    Cash in Hand           300

                           11500                          11500
```

```
                       Balance Sheet of A Brown
                          as at 9 March 19__

    Capital and Liabilities  £      £       Assets              £      £
    Capital                         6000    Fixed assets

    Long-term liabilities                   Premises            3000
      Bank loan              4000           Fixtures and fittings 1200
      Motor loan             6000           Motor vehicles      8000
                                   10000                              12200

    Current liabilities                     Current assets
                                            Stock               1400
      Creditors                     750     Debtors              400
                                            Cash at Bank        2450
                                            Cash in Hand         300
                                                                       4550

                                   16750                              16750
```

REVIEW QUIZ

True or false?

1 Profit increases capital.

2 The net profit is profit before expenses have been deducted.

3 Drawings are pictures painted by the owner.

4 A debtor is someone we owe money to.

5 The more liquid an asset, the harder it is to turn into cash.

Complete the blanks . . .

6 The formula for a balance sheet is

Capital + ... = ...

7 Debts which have to be paid back fairly quickly are called

....

8 When an asset falls in value over a period the technical term
is ....

Work it out

9 Peter Riley has the following items in his balance sheet on
31 May 19--

Cash at Bank £5400; Motor Vehicles £12 000; Stock £5200;
Bank Loan £6000; Debtors £1400; Creditors £2100; Cash in
Hand £750; Fixtures and Fittings £3100; Shop Premises
£5000.

Write up his balance sheet, classifying the items correctly
into assets and liabilities and calculate his capital.

10 During the first week of June, Peter Riley:

a paid one of his creditors £800 by cheque.
b received payment of £700 from one of his debtors which
he banked.
c sold a further £2000 of stock on credit.
d bought £1400 of stock and paid by cheque.
e bought a new electronic till for £1000 which he paid for by
cheque.
f paid one of his creditors £150 from the cash he keeps on
the premises.

Write up his balance sheet after the above transactions have
all been completed.

11 From the work you have done so far, can you state
 – why organisations keep accounts
 – the obligations (in relation to completing legal returns
and providing other information) of an accounts
department.

Section 2 – Double-entry book-keeping

INTRODUCTION TO DOUBLE ENTRY

Although drawing up a new balance sheet after every transaction gives an accurate picture of the state of the company, it would obviously be impractical in real life. Companies carry out hundreds or thousands of transactions every day and many people need to be able to work on the accounts at the same time.

We therefore need to have a system where the transactions can be recorded in their own accounts quickly and simply. A system which is easy to check and which, at the end of any given period, will enable us to work out how much profit the company has made and draw up a balance sheet. This system is known as **double-entry book-keeping**.

How it works

You have already been using double entry. You have seen that every transaction has *two* effects and has therefore to be entered twice. This is *double entry*.

DOUBLE-ENTRY BOOK-KEEPING – A CASE STUDY

For this section we are going to follow the progress of Sarah Barnes. Sarah has inherited some money from an elderly aunt and has decided to use this to open her own business. She is going to rent premises and start her own secretarial and duplicating service and also hopes to sell office supplies.

Sarah has already attended a book-keeping course and the first thing she does is to buy herself a Ledger – a specially printed and ruled book in which accounts can be recorded – in which she can enter all her transactions.

She knows she must:

- make out each account on a separate page, with the title at the top
- make *two* entries for every transaction
- use the *left* side of the page for **debits**
- use the *right* side of the page for **credits**
- make the opposite entry for an item which is an asset to that which is a liability. She uses the following chart to help her remember what to do.

<table>
<tr><td colspan="2" align="center">Liabilities or Capital</td></tr>
<tr><td>DR</td><td align="right">CR</td></tr>
<tr><td align="center">DECREASE = DEBIT SIDE   INCREASE = CREDIT SIDE</td><td></td></tr>
<tr><td>↓</td><td align="right">↑</td></tr>
</table>

Liabilities or Capital
DR   CR
        DECREASE = DEBIT SIDE   INCREASE = CREDIT SIDE
    ↓   ↑

Assets
DR   CR
        INCREASE = DEBIT SIDE   DECREASE = CREDIT SIDE
    ↑   ↓

CHECK IT YOURSELF

It is doubtful if you can remember the chart at this stage – and you will probably need to refer to it often. Copy the chart down onto a piece of card which you can keep nearby until you can work easily without it.

Stage 1 – Starting up

Sarah has put her capital into the bank at this stage. She therefore makes out two pages – one for Capital and one for Bank.

She knows she has to:

- write the date first
- write a description next – this is the name of the account containing the opposite entry to the one she is now making
- enter the amount.

Below are shown her entries. Note that we are showing them one under the other to save space.

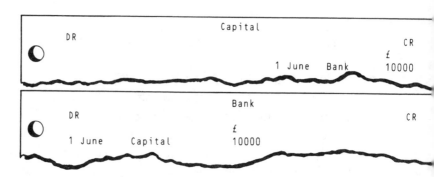

SPECIAL NOTE

When you use ledger paper you will see it is divided down the middle so that the entries are easy to make.

CHECK IT YOURSELF

Compare the entries above with the instructions on your chart. Are they correct?

Capital has increased. This is therefore entered on the *credit* side. **Bank** (an *asset*) has also increased. This is therefore on the *debit* side.

Stage 2 – Buying for cash

Sarah now goes out and spends £1000 on fixtures and fittings. She pays by cheque.

She needs to start a new account now titled Fixtures and Fittings. Work out, with the help of your chart, which side her entries should be on. Do this *before* you look at the completed accounts below.

Were you correct?

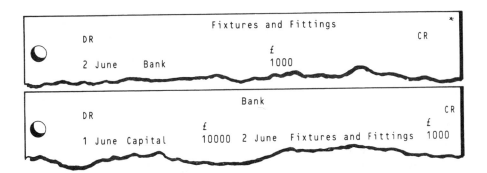

```
                    Fixtures and Fittings                      *
    DR                                              CR
                                £
    2 June    Bank             1000
```

```
                         Bank                          CR
    DR
                    £                                  £
    1 June Capital  10000  2 June  Fixtures and Fittings  1000
```

Her fixtures and fittings (an *asset*) have *increased* – the entry is therefore on the *debit* side.

Her bank account (which is also an *asset*) has *decreased* so the entry is on the *credit* side.

SPECIAL NOTE

As you can see Sarah has written the entry to pay for her fixtures and fittings on the bank account, alongside her original entry for capital.

All the entries for one account are kept on the same page, written either alongside, or underneath one another.

Stage 3 – Buying on credit

Sarah now goes out to buy some office equipment – a fax machine, a photocopier and a word processor. Because these cost her £5000 she decides to buy them on credit. She has now gained a **creditor** (a liability) whom she must repay in the future.

She needs to open an account in the name of this creditor – in this case Business Machines Ltd and another account to record her equipment.

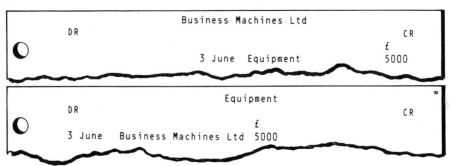

Hopefully you can already understand why the entries have been made like this.

Her equipment is an *asset*, it has *increased*, therefore it is a *debit* entry.

Business Machines Ltd are a *liability*, because they are a creditor. This entry also records an *increase* (in Sarah's debt to them) and therefore it is a *credit* entry.

Stage 4 – Paying creditors

Sarah's father thinks her credit with Business Machines Ltd is too high. He suggests she pays them £500 to reduce her credit a little. He also suggests she takes £300 out of the bank in cash to keep on the premises. Can you work out the entries she made?

The accounts are on page 144. Did you work them out correctly?

Paying Business Machines Ltd means she is reducing a liability. Therefore the payment is recorded on the *debit* side.

Starting a Cash account (an *asset*) and *increasing* this from zero to £300 means the entry must be on the *debit* side.

Both payments have been made by *reducing* an *asset* – her money in the bank. These entries have therefore been made on the *credit* side.

CHECK IT YOURSELF

On a sheet of ledger paper copy out the accounts Sarah has opened which are marked with an asterisk (*) in the text (the latest version of the account).

Leave enough space within each for more entries to be added.

Note that she has six accounts so far – Capital, Fixtures and Fittings, Equipment, and the three shown on page 144 – Business Machines Ltd, Cash and Bank.

Ask your tutor to check they are correct before you carry on.

TEST YOURSELF

Decide in each of the cases below whether the entry should be made on the debit or the credit side.

1	Sarah buys a car for £3000 (open Car account – an asset).	DR or CR
	She pays by cheque (this reduces her Bank account).	DR or CR
2	Sarah buys some display stands (increasing her Fittings).	DR or CR
	She pays £200 for them in cash (reducing her Cash account).	DR or CR
3	She buys an answering machine for £200 (increasing Equipment)	DR or CR
	which she buys on credit from Automation Ltd (another creditor).	DR or CR
4	She takes a further £300 out of the bank (reduces Bank)	DR or CR
	to keep on the premises (increases Cash).	DR or CR
5	She pays another £500 by cheque (reduces Bank)	DR or CR
	to Business Machines Ltd (reducing this creditor).	DR or CR

Complete this test before you read the next section.

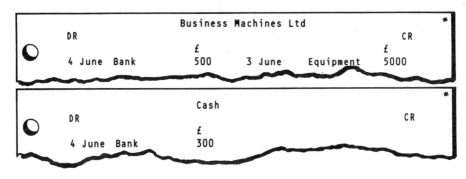

Business Machines Ltd				
DR				CR
	£			£
4 June Bank	500	3 June	Equipment	5000

Cash		
DR		CR
	£	
4 June Bank	300	

Bank				
DR				CR
	£			£
1 June Capital	10000	2 June	Fixtures and Fittings	1000
		4 June	Business Machines Ltd	500
		4 June	Cash	300

CHECK IT YOURSELF

Your answers to the Test Yourself on the previous page should have been:

1	debit Car account	credit Bank account
2	debit Fixtures and Fittings	credit Cash account
3	debit Equipment	credit Automation Ltd
4	debit Cash account	credit Bank account
5	debit Business Machines Ltd account	credit Bank account

Hopefully you were right every time. Now write up all these entries in the correct accounts. Make out new accounts where necessary and date all your entries 7 June.

Check your work with your tutor before you carry on.

Stage 5 – Buying stock

Sarah now goes out to buy some stock for her shop. She knows she must treat this differently because she intends to resell her stock to her customers. It is therefore a *current* asset, *not* a *fixed* asset, (like her car, equipment and fixtures and fittings).

Purchases is the name we give to stock bought for resale
Sales is the name we give to stock which is resold.

Sarah buys £500 of stock on 8 June and pays by cheque. Her bank
account therefore goes down and must be *credited*. Her purchases
go up and must be *debited*.

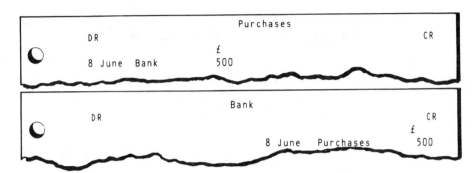

On 9 June she buys £1000 of stock from a company called Allwrite
Ltd. This time she buys her stock on credit. On this occasion her
purchases have again increased and so must be *debited*. Her
account with a new creditor (a liability) has increased, therefore
this must be *credited*.

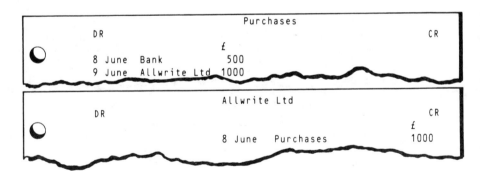

Stage 6 – Selling stock

Sarah now opens for business. On the first day she sells £50 of
her stock for cash and immediately banks this money.

She now opens a sales account. Her asset of stock has decreased
by selling the goods so she must *credit* her sales account.

Her bank account has increased by £50 so she must *debit* this
account.

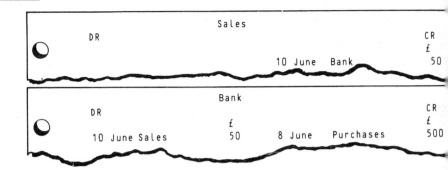

```
                    Sales
    DR                                              CR
                                                    £
                          10 June   Bank            50

                    Bank
    DR                                              CR
                          £                         £
    10 June Sales         50    8 June   Purchases  500
```

The following day Sarah sells £250 of goods to D Wright and agrees he can settle his account later. D Wright therefore becomes Sarah's first **debtor**.

Again Sarah's asset of stock has decreased so she must *credit* her sales account.

D Wright, as a debtor, is an asset. His debt to Sarah is an increase in an asset so she must *debit* his account.

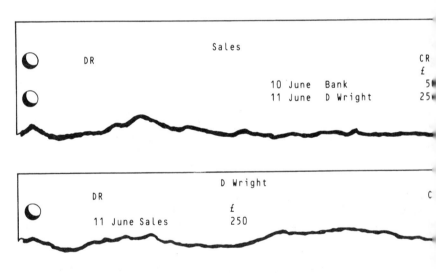

```
                        Sales
    DR                                              CR
                                                    £
                          10 June   Bank            5
                          11 June   D Wright        25

                      D Wright
    DR                                              C
                          £
    11 June Sales         250
```

CHECK IT YOURSELF

D Wright calls back on 13 June and pays £75 off his account which Sarah banks. Can you work out the entries which must be made?

The answer is at the top of the next page. Were you correct?

		D Wright					
DR							CR
			£				£
11 June	Sales		250	13 June	Bank		75

		Bank					
DR							CR
			£				£
10 June	Sales		50	8 June	Purchases		500
13 June	D Wright		75				

✓ TEST YOURSELF

Sarah buys and sells several goods over the next few days. From the list below can you work out which account would be credited and which would be debited for each transaction?

14 June Sarah sells £200 of stock for cash and banks the money.

17 June She buys £400 of stock from Business Machines Ltd on credit.
She also sells £150 of stock but decides to keep this in cash.

18 June Sarah pays Allwrite Ltd £100 by cheque.
She sells a further £100 of stock to D Wright on credit.

19 June Sarah buys £300 of stock and pays by cheque.
D Wright pays £150 off his account by cheque.

20 June Sarah pays Business Machines Ltd £100 by cheque.
She sells £200 of stock to K Noble on credit.

Check all your answers with your tutor.

✓ TEST YOURSELF

Practise entering purchases and sales. Starting with new accounts, enter the following:

1 June buy stock worth £2000 and pay by cheque
sell stock worth £500 and bank money received

2 June buy stock from Business Machines Ltd – cost £1500 – on credit

3 June sell stock worth £600 to K Noble on credit

9 June pay Business Machines Ltd by cheque – £500
sell stock worth £200 and keep this money in cash

Double-entry book-keeping 147

18 June   sell stock worth £800 to K Noble on credit

22 June   pay Business Machines Ltd by cheque – £300
           buy stock worth £100 and pay in cash

28 June   receive cheque from K Noble for £500.

Check all your entries with your tutor.

Stage 7 – Returns

On 23 June K Noble sends back £30 of goods which were
damaged. To cope with this situation Sarah needs to make out a
new account – **returns inwards**. Stock which has previously been
sold has been returned and come back *in* to the company.

K Noble now owes Sarah £30 less. This decreases his debt to her
(an *asset*) so must be entered as a *credit*. Her stock has increased
by these returns (just as if she had purchased more goods),
therefore the Returns Inwards account must be *debited*.

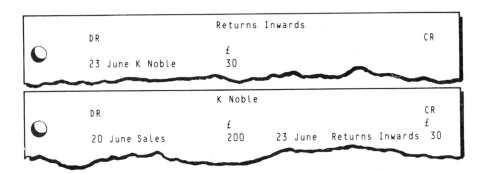

On 24 June Sarah buys £200 of stock from Datahouse Ltd on
credit. The next day she realises several items are faulty and
sends these back to the company. These items cost her £25. She
now needs to open a **returns outwards** account. Stock she has
bought has been sent back *out* of her company.

CHECK IT YOURSELF
Can you make out the accounts to show her transactions on 24 June?

We now need to record her returns. Her liability to Datahouse Ltd has now decreased by £25, this must therefore be entered as a *debit*.

Her Returns Outwards represent a decrease in her stock (an asset). This must therefore be entered as a *credit*.

The accounts are shown below:

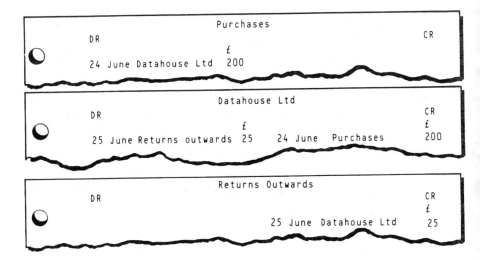

TEST YOURSELF

Make out accounts (start with new entries) for each of the transactions shown below:

1 July   Sarah buys £500 stock on credit from Allwrite Ltd.
　　　　She sells £600 of stock for cash and banks the money.

2 July   Sarah returns £50 of stock to Allwrite Ltd because it was damaged.
　　　　Sarah buys £400 of stock and pays by cheque.

3 July   D Webster buys £250 of stock on credit.
　　　　Sarah buys £200 of stock from Datahouse Ltd on credit.

4 July   D Webster returns £20 of goods which were faulty.
　　　　Sarah returns £10 of stock to Datahouse Ltd.

SPECIAL NOTE

There is obviously a very close link between *accounts* and *business documents*.

When we **purchase** goods we expect to receive an **invoice**.

When we **sell** goods we will send out an **invoice**.

When we **return** goods **outwards** we expect to receive a **credit note**.

When we receive **returns inwards** we will send out a **credit note**.

CHECK IT YOURSELF

Work out the business documents which will be sent and received to link with the transactions you have just entered.

Check your answers with your tutor.

Stage 8 – Expenses

Sarah has obviously many expenses involved with running her business. She makes telephone calls, pays her rent, advertises her business in the local paper, buys stationery and takes out insurance against fire and theft. She also wants to take money out of the business for her own private use (to live on!). These are called **drawings**.

Every time she pays a bill for any of these expenses, and when she draws money out for her own use, she *decreases* the amount of money she holds in cash or has in the bank. Therefore her assets of cash or bank must be *credited*.

On the opposite side, each of her expenses must be listed in its own account. Every time she pays a bill she is *increasing* the amount she spends on that particular expense. The expense account is therefore *debited*.

CHECK IT YOURSELF

On 10 July Sarah pays £100 rent, £65 telephone bill and £20 insurance premium. She pays all these bills by cheque. Can you work out her entries?

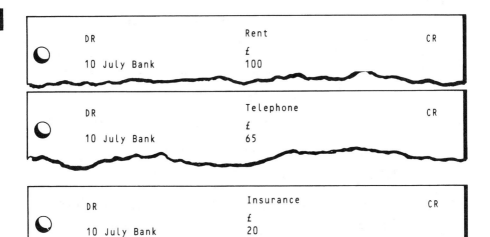

DR	Rent	CR
	£	
10 July Bank	100	

DR	Telephone	CR
	£	
10 July Bank	65	

DR	Insurance	CR
	£	
10 July Bank	20	

Draw up her bank entries **before** you read the next section. You will find the answer on the next page.

TEST YOURSELF

You should now be able to deal with a wide range of transactions. You can record:

- purchasing of fixed assets for cash and on credit (Stages 1, 2 and 3)
- paying creditors (Stage 4)
- buying and selling stock for cash and on credit (Stages 5 and 6)
- Returns Inwards and Returns Outwards (Stage 7)
- recording expenses (Stage 8).

Put this knowledge to good use by recording various transactions undertaken by Sarah during September. Start each account as a new entry.

1 Sept   Sarah buys £500 stock on credit from Miniprint Ltd.

3 Sept   She sells £400 stock for cash and banks the money.

5 Sept   She takes £100 out of the bank to keep in cash on the premises.

10 Sept   P Knights buys £175 of goods from Sarah on credit.

12 Sept   Sarah returns £25 of faulty goods to Miniprint Ltd.

15 Sept   Sarah buys £40 of stationery and pays in cash.

16 Sept   Sarah pays Miniprint by cheque – £100

18 Sept   P Knights buys more goods on credit worth £235.

19 Sept   P Knights returns £35 of goods which were damaged.

22 Sept   Sarah draws out £75 from the bank to keep in cash.

25 Sept   Sarah pays Miniprint Ltd another £150 by cheque.

26 Sept   Sarah sells £600 of goods for cash and banks the money.

27 Sept   P Knights sends a cheque for £300.

30 Sept   Sarah buys £200 of stock and pays by cheque.

Check all your answers with your tutor before you go any further.
Here is the answer to the Check it Yourself section on page 151.

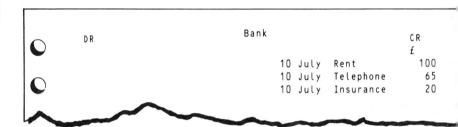

DR			Bank		CR
					£
		10 July	Rent		100
		10 July	Telephone		65
		10 July	Insurance		20

Stage 9 – Balancing accounts

To be able to work out exactly what Sarah owes other people,
what they owe her, and how much she has in cash and at the bank
we need to *balance* the accounts.

By balancing the account we can work out how much someone
owes Sarah. We will assume she had a customer called P Banks in
August who bought goods from her on credit, returned some
goods and paid for others. At the end of August his account looks
like this:

			P Banks				
DR							CR
			£				£
1 Aug	Sales		200	5 Aug	Returns Inwards		25
8 Aug	Sales		650	12 Aug	Bank		450
14 Aug	Sales		230	24 Aug	Bank		200
25 Aug	Sales		365				

Debit balances

To balance an account you must:

- add up the side which has the greater total (for a debit balance this will be the debit side)

- draw a total line across the columns, after leaving a blank line for the final balance entry on the opposite side

- enter the larger total figure *in pencil*

- add up the opposite side (the smaller total)

- deduct this from the larger total and enter the difference on the balance line, still in pencil, with the letters c/d to show that this figure will be **carried down**

- check that your final totals are equal at both sides

- when you are certain you are correct write the figures in ink

- carry down your balance to the *opposite side* with the letters b/d to denote it has been **brought down**.

P Banks' balanced account is shown below.

```
                              P Banks
    DR                                                        CR
                               £                               £
    1  Aug  Sales            200    5  Aug  Returns Inwards    25
    8  Aug  Sales            650   12  Aug  Bank              450
    14 Aug  Sales            230   24  Aug  Bank              200
    25 Aug  Sales            365   31  Aug  Balance c/d       770
                           ─────                            ─────
                            1445                             1445

    1  Sept Balance  b/d     770    A DEBIT BALANCE ENDS ON THE
                                    DEBIT SIDE
```

TEST YOURSELF

What business document would we issue to P Banks at the end of August which is a copy of this account, and tells him how much he still owes?

Credit balances

If we still owe someone money then the balance will be shown on the *opposite* side. We can see this by looking at Sarah's account with one of her suppliers – Quickfile Ltd – at the end of August.

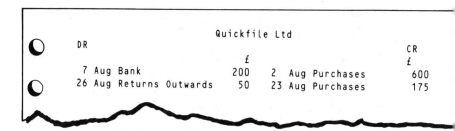

```
                              Quickfile Ltd
    DR                                                           CR
                                    £                             £
    7 Aug Bank                     200   2  Aug Purchases        600
   26 Aug Returns Outwards          50  23  Aug Purchases        175
```

Can you balance this account yourself before you continue? You can check your answer on page 156.

Remember – always add up the larger side first.

SPECIAL NOTE

Always make sure you carry down the **balance** figure – not the total by mistake.

TEST YOURSELF

What document can we expect to receive from Quickfile Ltd at the end of the month to show identical entries to those shown above?

CHECKING BUSINESS DOCUMENTS

Hopefully you have realised that we will *issue* statements at the end of the month to all our customers who still *owe* us money. The statement will be a copy of their accounts entries for that month.

Equally we will *receive* statements from our suppliers. These must be carefully checked against our creditors' accounts so that we can make certain we are not being wrongly charged.

Obviously on a statement the words Returns Outwards and Returns Inwards are not used. These entries would be noted as Credit Notes.

TEST YOURSELF

At the end of Stage 8 you produced a number of accounts for Sarah Barnes. You should have checked these with your tutor to make sure they were correct.

If you made a mess of any of them rewrite these neatly now.

Complete Sarah's books for September by:

- balancing all her accounts as at 30 September and carrying down the balances on 1 October
- noting down the documents you will expect to issue and receive
- working out what is the *total* amount owed by Sarah at the end of the month to her suppliers
- working out how much money is still owing to her
- if you found you were carrying forward larger and larger balances each month for one particular customer what would this mean? What action would you advise Sarah to take?

Check all your answers, and your balanced accounts, with your tutor.

Aged Debtors' Account

Ever-increasing balances would mean that the customer is not paying his or her bills. Action to take includes sending reminders and stopping further credit – Sarah should introduce a credit control system to keep a check on this (see pages 8 and 9).

To keep Sarah up-to-date on such information, an Aged Debtors' Account is produced each month from the balances carried forward. An example was shown in the chapter on Documents Relating to Goods and Services on page 10. Look back at this now and see how it relates to the work you have just done.

SECTION REVIEW

Having completed this section, you should now be able to:

1 Explain the principles of double-entry book-keeping.

2 Make double entries for
- assets bought for cash or on credit
- paying creditors
- buying and selling stock (cash or credit)
- returning goods and receiving returned goods
- expenses.

3 Balance accounts accurately.

4 Explain the relationship between outstanding balances, credit control and the aged debtors' account.

5 Explain the relationship between accounts documents and double-entry book-keeping.

Here is the answer to the question on page 154.

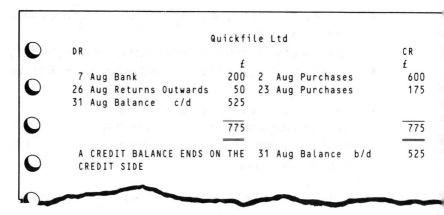

```
                        Quickfile Ltd
   DR                                                        CR
                             £                                £
    7 Aug Bank               200   2  Aug Purchases          600
   26 Aug Returns Outwards    50  23  Aug Purchases          175
   31 Aug Balance    c/d     525

                             ───                             ───
                             775                             775
                             ═══                             ═══
   A CREDIT BALANCE ENDS ON THE  31 Aug Balance    b/d       525
   CREDIT SIDE
```

REVIEW QUIZ

True or False?

1   The left side of the page is used to record debits.

2   Fixtures and fittings are classed as current assets.

3   Buying stock is recorded under Stock Inwards.

4   A creditor is a liability because one day he must be repaid.

5   A credit balance at the end of the month means we still owe that person money.

Complete the blanks...

6   If an asset increases it is entered on the .... side.

7   When customers return faulty goods to us these are recorded in the .... account.

8   When we record payment on an expense involved in operating the business, eg advertising, this is entered on the .... side of that particular expense account.

Work it out

9 Complete the following:

	Account to be debited	Account to be credited
Bought £1000 stock on credit from Barnes Ltd		
Paid £75 wages in cash		
Owner withdrew £100 from bank for own use		
Sold £150 stock, paid by cheque		
Returned £150 of faulty goods to Barnes Ltd		
Paid rates by cheque – £300		
Bought equipment for £500, paid by cheque		
Paid £200 to Barnes Ltd		
Sold £500 on credit to P Slater		
P Slater returns £50 of faulty goods		
P Slater pays £200 in cash		

10 Complete double entry accounts for each of the following transactions and balance off the accounts at the end of the month.

The transactions are divided up into four weeks in October. You might find it easier to enter one week to begin with and check your entries before you carry on.

Week 1

4 Oct   Start business with £15 000 capital in the bank
5 Oct   Buy equipment worth £2500 and pay by cheque
6 Oct   Buy stock for £600 and pay by cheque
7 Oct   Pay rent – £200 – by cheque
8 Oct   Buy stock worth £2000 on credit from Electrix Ltd

Week 2

11 Oct   Return £50 of damaged stock to Electrix Ltd
12 Oct   Sell stock for £900 and bank cheque received

13 Oct   Sell £1000 of stock on credit to J Anderson
14 Oct   Sell £60 of stock and keep cash on premises
15 Oct   Pay cheque to Electrix for £1000

Week 3

18 Oct   Buy additional £3000 of stock on credit from Electrix
19 Oct   Return damaged stock worth £35 to Electrix Ltd
20 Oct   Sell further £1750 of stock on credit to J Anderson
21 Oct   J Anderson returns damaged stock worth £45
22 Oct   Withdraw £200 from bank to keep as cash on premises

Week 4

25 Oct   Buy additional equipment for £1500 by cheque
26 Oct   Receive cheque from J Anderson for £2000
27 Oct   Buy stock for £400 and pay by cheque
28 Oct   Sell stock value £700 and bank cheque received
29 Oct   Pay rent – £200 – by cheque

11   From the work you have just carried out, what do you consider to be the main principles of double-entry book-keeping?

Discuss your answers with your tutor.

Section 3 – Books of Account – Ledgers, Day Books, the Cash Book and the Journal

DIVIDING THE LEDGER

As Sarah Barnes's business grows she employs staff to help her run the business. She soon discovers that having all her accounts in one Ledger is not satisfactory because:

- the Ledger is getting very crowded with too many accounts in it
- only one person can work on the accounts, or refer to them, at once.

The only answer is to divide the ledger – and have separate books for different types of accounts. She decides to:

- have one book for her customers' personal accounts. This is called the **Sales Ledger**.
- have one book for her suppliers' personal accounts. This is called the **Purchases Ledger**.

- have a book which will record the receiving and paying out of money both by cheque and in cash. This is called the **Cash Book**.
- keep the rest of the accounts in the **General Ledger**. This would therefore include:
  - the Sales account
  - the Purchases account
  - Returns Inwards
  - Returns Outwards
  - Expenses
  - Fixed Assets.

SPECIAL NOTE
In some organisations the Purchases Ledger is known as the **Bought Ledger**, and the General Ledger is referred to as the **Nominal (or Real) Ledger**.

TEST YOURSELF
After Sarah has reorganised her books, in which book would you look to find:
1 details of money paid into the bank
2 details of all the goods bought this month from Allwrite Ltd
3 details of all expenditure on stationery
4 details of all the goods sold to K Noble this month
5 details of any returns made by Sarah to her suppliers
6 details of expenditure on new office equipment.

CHECK IT YOURSELF
- If the business grew still further and required more than one Sales or Purchases Ledger, how could these be sub-divided?
- Which book still holds the most accounts, and therefore still might become full very quickly?

DAY BOOKS

The Sales Ledger or Purchases Ledger could easily be sub-divided on an alphabetical basis (even to the point where there was one book for each letter of the alphabet).

However, every time an entry is made in the Sales or Purchases Ledger an *opposite* entry is made under Sales or Purchases in the General Ledger. Therefore this book could quickly become very full indeed.

To solve this problem Sarah introduces one other set of books. These will not be part of the double entry system but will act like a diary, listing sales or purchases made so that just the total can be transferred to the General Ledger at the end of each month.

This will mean that space will be saved in the General Ledger and fewer people will constantly be wanting to work in the General Ledger at the same time.

She will call these two new books
- the **Sales Day Book** and
- the **Purchases Day Book**.

How it works

Below is shown Sarah's Sales Day Book, Sales Ledger and General Ledger for October. You can see from this how only the *total* of the entries in the Sales Day Book are transferred to the General Ledger at the end of the month.

```
                        SALES DAY BOOK
    Date      Customer                    Invoice No        Amount

    1   Oct   B Taylor                    27384             £1250
    7   Oct   Patel & Woods Ltd           27385             £1500
    16  Oct   Technico Electronics        27386              £755
    26  Oct   B Taylor                    27387              £500

              Transferred to Sales account                 £4005
```

```
                        SALES LEDGER
    DR                    B Taylor                        CR
                             £
    1   Oct Sales          1250
    26  Oct Sales           500
```

```
                        SALES LEDGER
    DR                 Patel & Woods Ltd                  CR
                             £
    7   Oct Sales          1500
```

```
                        SALES LEDGER
    DR                Technico Electronics                CR
                             £
    26  Oct Sales           500
```

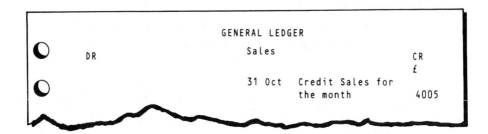

```
                        GENERAL LEDGER
  ◐          DR              Sales                        CR
                                                          £
  ◐                         31 Oct    Credit Sales for
                                         the month        4005
```


FOLIO COLUMNS

Sarah is pleased with her new system until staff start to complain that when they look up one side of an entry it can take them ages to find the opposite entry, especially when they have to look through the whole of the Sales Ledger or the General Ledger to find one particular account.

They suggest that the way to solve this problem would be by using **folio columns**. By adding an extra column in each of the books, the name of the book where the opposite entry is to be found can be entered, plus the page number. The book name can be entered in abbreviated form to save space, eg:

CB = Cash Book   Therefore CB 22 = Cash Book page 22
GL = General Ledger Therefore GL 47 = General Ledger page 47

CHECK IT YOURSELF

What do you think the following abbreviations represent?

- SL 62
- PL 10
- SDB 24
- PDB 70

SPECIAL NOTE

The letter *C* in a folio column stands for **contra**. This abbreviation is used when both sides of the double-entry are made in the same account.

CHECK IT YOURSELF

What *other* advantage can you think of for using folio columns besides the fact that staff can find accounts more easily?

How it works

Following this paragraph is Sarah's Purchases Day Book, her Purchases Ledger and General Ledger for November – the month she started using folio columns. She is pleased with the new system and its other major advantage – that it acts as a check that the double entry has been made. Only when the double entry has been completed is the folio column completed – an empty folio column will therefore show that only half of the entry has been made. This system of using one book to enter the items to the other account, is known as **posting** the items.

```
                    PURCHASES DAY BOOK                    Page 10

  Date    Supplier              Invoice No   Folio        Amount

  1  Nov Allwrite Ltd          KL/2839      PL 04         £1800
  8  Nov Datahouse Ltd         P/2817247    PL 42          £650
  18 Nov Allwrite Ltd          KL/3082      PL 04          £590
  26 Nov Miniprint Ltd         029381/3     PL 31         £2050

       Transferred to Purchases Account   GL 48          £5090
```

```
                    PURCHASES LEDGER
                      Allwrite Ltd                Page 4
       DR                                                  CR
                                                           £
                         1 Nov    Purchases PDB 10       1800
                         18 Nov   Purchases PDB 10        590
```

```
                    PURCHASES LEDGER          Page 42
       DR               Datahouse Ltd                CR
                                                     £
                         8 Nov   Purchases PDB 10    590
```

```
                    PURCHASES LEDGER          Page 31
       DR               Miniprint Ltd                CR
                                                     £
                         26 Nov   Purchases PDB 10   2050
```

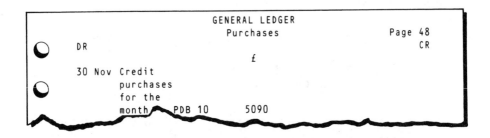

```
                        GENERAL LEDGER
                          Purchases                    Page 48
    DR                                                      CR
                              £
   30 Nov  Credit
           purchases
           for the
           month    PDB 10      5090
```

CHECK IT YOURSELF

Follow carefully all the entries shown above. See how the page numbers are entered in the folio column, in each case showing where the other half of the double entry can be found.

Talk through the transactions with your tutor if you have any difficulties.

SPECIAL NOTE

All purchases and sales are entered in their respective accounts *after* allowing for any discounts. Therefore, if Sarah is charged £1000 for goods less 10% trade discount, all the entries for that purchase are entered as £900 – the price she actually pays. Similarly if Sarah gives discount to her own customers, all their entries show the *net* amount of the invoice – the amount less discount.

TEST YOURSELF

Sarah has sold the following goods during November: **Invoice No**

2 Nov	To B Noble, goods worth £850 less 15% trade discount	72971
10 Nov	To Technico Electronics, goods worth £1420 less 12½% trade discount	72972
17 Nov	To D Wilinski, goods worth £500 less 7½% trade discount	72973
22 Nov	To B Noble, goods worth £1520 less 15% trade discount	72974
29 Nov	To B Taylor, goods worth £1622 less 10% trade discount	72975

Enter all these transactions on page 15 of the Sales Day Book.

Note that the Sales Ledger page numbers are as follows:

B Noble – page 12   Technico Electronics – page 27   D Wilinski – page 16
B Taylor – page 43

Enter the transactions in the appropriate customer accounts and then complete the Sales account on page 32 of the General Ledger at the end of the month.

Check your work with your tutor when you have finished.

RETURNS DAY BOOKS

The idea of using Day Books is so successful that Sarah decides to expand the system and introduce two other books:

- a **Returns Inwards Day Book** and
- a **Returns Outwards Day Book**.

Again the same procedure will be used. All the returns for the month received from customers will be posted in the customer's account in the Sales Ledger and listed in the Returns Inwards Day Book. At the end of the month just the *total* from the Returns Inwards Day Book will be posted to the Returns Inwards account in the General Ledger.

All returns sent back to suppliers by Sarah will be entered in the appropriate supplier's account in the Purchases Ledger and listed in the Returns Outwards Day Book. Only the total in this book will be posted to the Returns Outwards account in the General Ledger.

How it works

```
                        RETURNS INWARDS DAY BOOK              Page 3

      Date    Customer                      Credit   Folio   Amount
                                            Note No           £


       1  Dec B Noble                        C156    SL 12     150
       7  Dec D Wilinski                     C157    SL 16      35
      13  Dec B Noble                        C158    SL 12      22
      22  Dec Technico Electronics Ltd       C159    SL 27      50

             Transferred to Returns Inwards Account  GL 86     257
```

```
                           GENERAL LEDGER
                           Returns Inwards                Page 86
      DR                        £                              CR
      31 Dec   Returns
               for the
               month     RI  3257
```

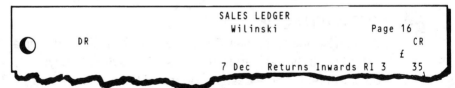

```
                        SALES LEDGER
            DR              B Noble               Page 12
                                                        CR
                                                    £
                         1 Dec   Returns Inwards RI 3    150
                        13 Dec   Returns Inwards RI 3     22


                        SALES LEDGER
                          Wilinski               Page 16
            DR                                          CR
                                                    £
                         7 Dec   Returns Inwards RI 3     35


                        SALES LEDGER
                   Technico Electronics Ltd      Page 27
            DR                                          CR
                                                    £
                        22 Dec   Returns Inwards RI 3     50
```

SPECIAL NOTE

It may help if you think of all Day Books as a kind of diary – listing the transactions which have occurred in date order.

TEST YOURSELF

Complete Sarah's Returns Outwards Day Book for December. Remember these are goods she has returned to her suppliers.

After you have listed them in the Day Book post them to the individual supplier's account in the Purchases Ledger. At the end of the month transfer the total listed in the day book to the Returns Outwards account in the General Ledger.

For your information you are up to page 6 in the Returns Outwards Day Book, and the Returns Outwards account is on page 88 of the General Ledger.

This month she has returned goods as follows:

3 Dec   Goods worth £87 to Allwrite Ltd (page 4 of the Purchases Ledger)
Their credit note number is CN/938

10 Dec   Goods worth £29 to Miniprint Ltd (page 31 of the Purchases Ledger)
Their credit note number is 4718

16 Dec   Goods worth £16 – again to Allwrite Ltd. Their credit note number is CN/946.

22 Dec   Goods worth £33 to Office Supplies Ltd (page 24 of the Purchases Ledger). Their credit note number is OS/1101

All these suppliers have given Sarah 10% discount. This must be allowed for on returns as well as on purchases!

THE CASH BOOK

Sarah now opens her new Cash Book, in which she will keep a record of all the cash and cheques she receives and pays out. This book will replace the Cash Account and Bank Account she used to keep in her ledger, when she was using one book for all her accounts. Sarah will therefore use a two column Cash Book – one column for the Cash Account and the other for the Bank Account.

Cash Book Entries

Money *received* goes on the left:
- the debit (DR) column(s)

Money *paid out* goes on the right:
- the credit (CR) column(s)

Cash received includes:
- payments received by the organisation in cash which will *not* be banked immediately
- cash taken out of the bank[++]

Cash paid out includes:
- cash transferred to the bank[+]
- cash payments made from cash kept on the premises

Bank received includes:
- payments received by the organisation in cash or by cheque and paid into the bank immediately
- cash paid into the bank which has been held in the cash account[+]

Bank paid out includes:
- cheques made out by the organisation for goods and supplies
- cheques made out for cash[++]

SPECIAL NOTE

⁺ These are the opposite side of the same thing! Cash taken out of the cash account and paid into the bank means

Bank account goes *up* (debit)   Cash account goes *down* (credit)

⁺⁺ In this case the reverse is true – when money is taken out of the bank for cash (eg cashing a cheque) then

Cash account goes *up* (debit)   Bank account goes *down* (credit)

eg Sarah's cash book for October is shown below:

```
                                    Cash Book
       DR                                                              CR
                    Cash   Bank                        Cash   Bank
       19__          £      £      19__                 £      £
       Oct  1  Balances b/d  350   4780   Oct  3  Wages               417
       Oct  4  D Wright      50           Oct 10  Travel       25
       Oct  9  Sales               490    Oct 15  Cash    C           100
       Oct 15  Bank    C    100           Oct 17  Wages               410
       Oct 23  Sales               530    Oct 25  Cleaner     50
       Oct 29  K Noble      80            Oct 30  Bank    C   150
       Oct 30  Cash    C           150
```

!

SPECIAL NOTE

- The first entry balances **b/d (brought down)** are the balances held in the cash account (money on the premises) and in the bank account at the beginning of the month.
- On 15th October we withdrew £100 cash out of the bank. The entry is therefore shown twice – the bank account as a credit, the cash account as a debit – both marked with the letter **C** for **contra**.
- On 30 October we paid £150 cash into the bank. This entry is also made twice – the bank account as a debit, the cash as a credit and also marked with a **C**.

- Only money which is going to be kept on the premises is entered into the cash account. Organisations do *not* enter money into the cash account one minute (as it is received) and transfer it to the bank account the next (as it is paid into the bank). This would make too much work. Money received which is to be paid into the bank immediately is entered straight into the bank column.

CHECK IT YOURSELF

Talk through all the transactions shown with your tutor and make sure you understand them.

TEST YOURSELF

Draw up a page of a cash book as shown above and enter Sarah's transactions during November:

		£
Nov 1	Balances brought forward from last month:	
	Cash	120
	Bank	3 450
Nov 2	Banked sales takings	620
Nov 6	Paid cleaner by cash	45
Nov 10	Withdrew cash from bank	150
Nov 17	Paid wages by cheque	350
Nov 23	Received cash from M Hussein	200
Nov 26	Paid travel expenses by cash	20
Nov 26	Banked sales takings	500
Nov 27	Banked £100 of the cash held by the organisation	100

Balancing the cash book

At the end of every month the **cash book** must be balanced and a new balance brought down. This is done in the same way that ledger accounts were balanced in the last section.

TEST YOURSELF

Can you recall how you balanced ledger accounts in the last section? Draw up a list of the key points you would need if you were showing someone how to balance an account for the first time.

The Balanced Cash Book

Below is Sarah's Cash Book for October, correctly balanced-off.

```
                                  Cash Book
DR                                                                    CR
                  Cash   Bank                         Cash   Bank
19__               £      £      19__                  £      £
Oct  1  Balances b/d  350   4780   Oct  3  Wages              417
Oct  4  D Wright      50          Oct 10  Travel       25
Oct  9  Sales              490    Oct 15  Cash     C          100
Oct 15  Bank     C    100          Oct 17  Wages             410
Oct 23  Sales             530    Oct 25  Cleaner     50
Oct 29  K Noble      80          Oct 30  Bank      C  150
Oct 30  Cash     C         150    Oct 30  Balance  c/d  355   5023

                     580   5950                        580   5950
                     ───   ────                        ───   ────
Nov  1  Balances b/d  355   5023
```

TEST YOURSELF

Balance off Sarah's Cash Book for November.

THE JOURNAL

Sarah's new Accounts Clerk suggests she needs to keep one other book – the **Journal**. This will also be used as a kind of diary, but this time will record all the transactions which cannot easily be recorded in any of the other books.

These include:

- purchase of *fixed* assets on credit (eg machinery, motor vehicles, fittings and fixtures)
- sales of *fixed* assets on credit (eg when selling a motor vehicle before buying a new one)
- writing off bad debts
- expenditure on expenses
- miscellaneous transfers (eg a business we deal with changes ownership)
- the correction of any errors
- any other miscellaneous transactions.

Opening entries

Before the Journal can be started opening entries need to be made to show the current situation. This is merely a list of the capital, liabilities and assets on the day the Journal is started. The information is obtained from current entries in the General Ledger, Sales and Purchases Ledger and the Cash Book.

Day-to-day entries

Day-to-day entries are made in the Journal by writing the names of the accounts involved and a *narrative* underneath – a description of the transaction itself. If any documents are available to give proof of what has happened the reference number of these is included.

Examples

1 A person who owes us £96 has been declared bankrupt. Because we will now not be paid by him this is a **bad debt** – a debt which must be written off because it will not be paid.

   The person's name is R Turnbull.

   The Journal entry will show:

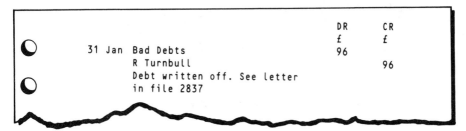

```
                                                    DR      CR
                                                    £       £
       31 Jan  Bad Debts                            96
               R Turnbull                                   96
               Debt written off. See letter
               in file 2837
```

2 Our organisation buys a new van at a cost of £9500 on credit from Axle Garages Ltd.

   The Journal entry will show:

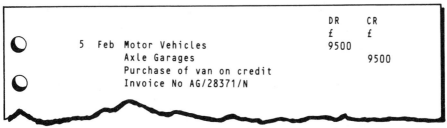

```
                                                    DR      CR
                                                    £       £
       5   Feb  Motor Vehicles                      9500
                Axle Garages                                9500
                Purchase of van on credit
                Invoice No AG/28371/N
```

3 On 17 February a bill is paid to Banks Motor Repairs for £455. An entry is made in the Journal to cover this expense. However, on 24 February it is discovered that £200 of this bill was for repairs to a private car belonging to the wife of the owner. This should therefore not have been paid through the

business. This error is also recorded in the Journal to show that the money has been repaid into the business by the owner.

		DR £	CR £
17 Feb	Motor Repairs	455	
	Bank		455
	Repairs as specified on Invoice No 48371		
24 Feb	Bank	200	
	Motor Repairs		200
	Repayment for repairs to private car listed in error on invoice No 48371		

TEST YOURSELF

Try writing up some Journal entries yourself. Remember to include:

- the date (all entries are made in date order, like a diary)
- the name of the account to be debited (this always comes first) and the amount
- the name of the account to be credited and the amount
- a simple narrative
- the reference number of any relevant documents.

1 March   We sell a motor vehicle to C Al-Said on credit for £5600. The sales agreement number is 4859.

5 March   We write off £350 owing to us by Nuttall & Sons as a bad debt. Nuttall's file is 2837.

12 March   The owner draws £800 out of the bank for his own use.

17 March   We pay an insurance premium of £250. Our policy reference is HK/09082/LPS

25 March   We buy additional office furniture from Designs Unlimited for £4250 on credit. The purchase agreement number is 7981.

30 March   It is discovered that £75 of the insurance premium we paid on 17 March relates to the owner's private insurance. He repays the money into the bank.

SECTION REVIEW

Having completed this section, you should now be able to:

1   Describe the different Books of Account kept by organisations.

2   Use folio columns and explain why these are adopted.

3   Explain the term **contra**.

4   Complete Sales and Purchases Day Books and Ledgers and transfer totals to the General (Nominal) Ledger.

5   Complete Returns Inwards and Outwards Day Book, make appropriate entries in the Sales or Purchases Ledger and transfer totals to the General (Nominal) Ledger.

6   Record income and expenditure in a Cash Book and balance.

7   Explain the use of a Journal and make simple entries.

8   Explain how a Sales and/or Purchases Ledger may be sub-divided and why this would be done.

REVIEW QUIZ

True or False?

1   Suppliers' personal accounts are recorded in the Purchases Ledger.

2   Purchases and sales are entered before allowing for trade discount.

3 In a Journal the name of the account to be credited is entered first.

4 Customers' personal accounts are recorded in the Sales Day Book.

5 Details of money paid into and out of the bank are kept in the General Ledger.

Complete the blanks...

6 Purchases and sales of fixed assets on credit are recorded in the .... and ....

7 Folio columns are used to record ....

8 Five books are used to record items in diary form. Only the .... are transferred to the General Ledger.

These five books are

....
....
....
....
....

Work it out

9 Sarah has bought the following goods on credit during January. Enter these transactions in the appropriate Day Book and Ledger. Show clearly which book you are writing in by your heading. At the end of the month make the appropriate entry in the General Ledger.

Invent consistent page numbers for your folio columns.

4 January   From Miniprint Ltd, goods worth £1450 less 10% trade discount – Invoice 4728

11 January   From Allwrite Ltd, goods worth £2100 less 12½% trade discount – Invoice 90281

13 January   From Datahouse Ltd, goods worth £20, no discount – Invoice 4282

15 January   From Miniprint Ltd, goods worth £1250 less
              10% trade discount – Invoice 4801

25 January   From Office Supplies Ltd, goods worth £890
              less 7½% trade discount – Invoice 20006

10   During January, Sarah returned some goods which were
         faulty or damaged. Her returns were

7 January   To Miniprint, goods worth £35

12 January   To Allwrite, goods worth £52

15 January   To Miniprint, goods worth £25

28 January   To Office Supplies Ltd, goods worth £72

Make these entries in the appropriate Day Book and Ledger
and at the end of the month make the appropriate entry in
the General Ledger. From your headings make it clear which
book you are writing in. Note that the discounts remain the
same as in question 9 and must be taken into account!

Assuming Sarah's address is 15 Castle Street, Caernarvon,
Gwynedd, North Wales EW16 8PJ, make out

- the credit note she can expect to receive from Miniprint
  Ltd. (Make out your own heading for Miniprint, whose
  offices are at 12 Bottomgate Row, Chester, CH3 9DK.
  Their telephone number is 0244-29384 and the credit
  note number is CR/382.)
- the statement she can expect to receive at the end of the
  month from Miniprint. Again invent your own heading
  and layout. The statement number is KN/39283.

11   Draw up a page of a cash book as shown in the chapter and
         enter the following transactions in the correct columns.
         Balance off your account at the end of the month and carry
         the new balance down.

March	1	Balances brought forward from last month	£
		Cash	402
		Bank	2784
March	2	Banked sales takings	542
March	7	Paid travel expenses by cash	70
March	9	Withdrew cash from bank	100
March	12	Banked sales takings	323
March	14	Paid wages by cheque	320
March	18	Paid cleaner in cash	60
March	21	K Robbins paid account in cash	242
March	24	J Munroe paid account in cash	152
March	28	Banked £400 of the cash held by the organisation	400

Section 4 – Final Accounts

THE TRIAL BALANCE

Usually once a month a **trial balance** is prepared. This is simply a *list* of all the balances – both debit and credit. If the entries have been correct then the *total* of the debit balances will equal the *total* of the credit balances.

If the two are not equal then this proves a mistake has been made. It may be that:

- the figures have not been added up or subtracted correctly
- figures have been transposed in one account (eg £7532 instead of £7352)
- the wrong figure has been carried down when completing the balancing, eg the total and not the balance figure.

However, you should note that there are certain types of errors which will not be highlighted, even when a trial balance is prepared.

CHECK IT YOURSELF

Can you think of the type of errors which will not be shown up in the trial balance and what could be done to find them?

Discuss this problem with your tutor – the answer is given later in this section.

TEST YOURSELF

In the section on double-entry book-keeping earlier in this chapter you practised balancing Sarah's accounts, in each case ending with a debit or credit balance.

Show you still remember how to do this by calculating the balance on each of the following accounts:

```
                              B NOBLE
DR                                                          CR
                              £                              £
  1 March   Sales          1450    3 March Returns Inwards   30
 10 March   Sales           800   11 March Bank            2200
 19 March   Sales          2300   24 March Bank             900
 28 March   Sales          1230

                             EQUIPMENT
DR                                                          CR
                              £                              £
  1 March   Designs UnLtd   1350
 15 March   Bank             550
```

You should have worked out a balance of

- £2650 for B Noble
- £1900 for Equipment

Both these should have been shown as *debit* balances – the balance being carried down to the debit side. Can you think why?

Both of these items are **assets** – B Noble is a debtor who owes £2650 at the end of March. Equipment is obviously an asset – it is a possession.

If **assets** show *debit* balances then **capital** and **liabilities** must show *credit* balances because:

Capital + Liabilities = Assets

Therefore:

Credit balances   = Debit balances

TEST YOURSELF

Do the following accounts result, usually, in credit or debit balances?

- Sales

- Purchases
- Expenses
- Returns Inwards
- Returns Outwards

If you find this difficult go back to where these accounts were introduced earlier in the chapter and work out on which side the balance would be. Discuss your answers with your tutor.

A simple example

After two months in business imagine that Sarah's books show the following balances:

Purchases £2500   Sales £3500   Allwrite Ltd |creditor| £2500

B Noble |debtor| £500   Business Machines Ltd |creditor| £5000

Fixtures and fittings £1000   Equipment £5000   Bank £11500

Cash £500   Capital £10000

We can now list these under whether each shows a credit or a debit balance as follows:

```
              Trial Balance as at 30 June 19__

                                    DR        CR
                                    £         £
        Purchases                 2500
        Sales                               3500
        Allwrite Ltd                        2500
        B Noble                    500
        Business Machines Ltd               5000
        Fixtures and Fittings     1000
        Equipment                 5000
        Bank                     11500
        Cash                       500
        Capital                            10000

                                 ─────      ─────
                                 21000      21000
                                 ═════      ═════
```

From this example you should be able to see – if you didn't work it out before – that sales are usually a *credit* item (because the asset of stock is decreasing every time we sell something) and purchases are a *debit* item.

For that reason, Returns Inwards gives us a *debit* balance and Returns Outwards a *credit* balance.

Expenses give a *debit* balance because, like all other assets, they involve expenditure by the business.

TEST YOURSELF

From the balances shown below draw up a trial balance for Sarah as at 31 July 19–.

Bank £5200   Motor vehicles £6500   Purchases £4250

Sales £6100   Miniprint Ltd [creditor] £2300   Quickfile [creditor] £890

B Noble [debtor] £2900   Equipment £5000   Fixtures and Fittings £1500

Returns Inwards £45   Returns Outwards £75   Rent £200   Telephone £70

Drawings £400   General Expenses £50   Cash £250   Capital £17000

If you do it correctly you should balance! Check your answer with your tutor.

Other types of errors

The various errors which you were asked to think of on page 176 and which would not be shown in the trial balance include:

- errors of omission (when an item is left out altogether)
- errors of entry (when one half of the entry is in the wrong account)
- compensating errors (both sides are wrong but cancel each other out).

A limited company is required by law to have its books **audited** every year. This means that accountants or auditors check every entry in the company's books, and this procedure will normally find errors which have been made.

A sole trader or a partnership completes the books and sends them to an accountant for the final accounts to be calculated. The accountant will check the books and query anything he is unsure about but he will not systematically check every transaction, as occurs when books are audited.

TEST YOURSELF

Enter up the following accounts for Javinda Hussein's first month in business during April of this year. Balance off the accounts and prepare a trial balance as at 30 April.

1 April   Started the company with capital of £10000 which she put into the bank.

3 April   Bought equipment for £3500 on credit from Barnes & Jackson Ltd.

4 April   Bought fixtures and fittings for £850 and paid by cheque.

5 April   Purchased goods on credit as follows – G H Booth £1450; P Sharples & Co £600; D Kenyon £2300.

8 April   Sold goods value £650 and put money into the bank.

10 April Sold goods on credit as follows – T Blackshaw £750; T Marshall £1200.

12 April Paid insurance by cheque £65.

15 April Paid G Booth £500 by cheque.

17 April Received payment from T Blackshaw – £500 cheque.

18 April Withdrew £200 from bank for cash and £500 as drawings.

19 April Bought goods for cash – £50.

23 April Paid cheques as follows – P Sharples & Co £200, D Kenyon £1000.

25 April Sold goods for cheque – £1500.

28 April Bought goods and paid by cheque – £1750

30 April Sold goods on credit – T Blackshaw £450
          Bought goods on credit – G H Booth £1000; D Kenyon £500

PROFIT AND LOSS

Most business owners are far more interested in whether they are making a healthy profit at the end of each month than whether the trial balance balances. Obviously they want their books to be kept accurately, otherwise the information they are given cannot be relied upon, but the vast majority of businesses are trading for just one reason – to make a profit.

Working out, in detail, the Profit and Loss account – technically called the Trading and Profit and Loss account – and the end of the year balance sheet is normally done by paid accountants. You would never be called upon to do this in normal office work unless you studied accounts to a much higher level than this chapter is designed to cover.

However, it is important that you see the contribution you will have made by extracting an accurate trial balance – the first step towards creating final accounts. There is a direct link between the trial balance you have just created and the balance sheets shown at the beginning of this chapter.

THE TRADING AND PROFIT AND LOSS ACCOUNTS

This is created partially from information contained in the trial balance.

First you must remember that there is a difference between **gross profit** and **net profit**. Can you remember what it is?

If you look back to pages 133–4 you will see these definitions given:

Gross profit • the difference between the cost price of stock and the selling price

Net profit • what is left out of the gross profit after all the expenses have been deducted, eg heating, rent etc.

SPECIAL NOTE

The definition for gross profit does *not* say that this is the difference between purchases and sales. The difference is simply that at the end of the year we will have bought stock, sold stock and *have some stock left over*.

The formula for gross profit is therefore:

Sales – Cost of goods sold = Gross profit
    [purchases – unsold stock]

The unsold stock is calculated by doing a stock inventory (usually once a year). When everything has been counted its value is calculated at the price the stock *cost*.

TEST YOURSELF

If Sarah's sales for the year are £59 500, her purchases £37 250 and her unsold stock had cost her £2250 to buy, what is her gross profit for the year?

Now work out what her net profit would be if her expenses for the year add up to £7600.

CHECK IT YOURSELF

You should see that there is a considerable difference between Sarah's gross profit and her net profit.

If you were Sarah's accountant and were giving her advice on how to increase her net profit next year, what suggestions would you give her?

Consider all the options open to her, and the advantages and disadvantages of each one.

Discuss your findings with your tutor.

SPECIAL NOTE

It is the **net profit** figure, not the gross profit, that Income Tax (in the case of sole traders and partnerships) and Corporation Tax (in the case of limited companies) is calculated on.

STOCK

After the Trading and Profit and Loss accounts have been calculated, the Sales and Purchases accounts are closed (as the balance in them has now been transferred to another account – the Profit and Loss account).

This leaves the balance of the closing stock for the year to be dealt with. This is now transferred to a new account – the Stock account – which is kept in the General Ledger, and the value of the stock is entered.

How it works

An example can easily be drawn up from the figures you worked out for Sarah in the last Test Yourself.

```
                              S Barnes
              Trading and Profit and Loss Account for
                     the year ended 31 March 19__

                                  £                              £
        Purchases                37250    Sales                59500
        Gross Profit    c/d      24500    Closing stock         2250
                                 -----                         -----
                                 61750                         61750
                                 =====                         =====

        Expenses*                 7600    Gross profit   b/d   24500
        Net profit               16900
                                 -----                         -----
                                 24500                         24500
                                 =====                         =====

                                 Sales
        DR                                                       CR
                                  £                              £
        31 March Trading Account 59500    31 March Balance b/d  59500
                                 =====                          =====

                               Purchases
        DR                                                       CR
                                  £                              £
                                          31 March Trading
        31 March Balance b/d     37250            account        250
                                 =====                           ===

                                 Stock
        DR                                                       CR
                                  £                              £
        31 March Trading account  2250
```

*In reality all the different expenses, rent, telephone etc would be listed separately.

! SPECIAL NOTE

A **non**-profit making organisation, such as a trade union or a sports club will not issue Trading and Profit and Loss accounts – for obvious reasons! Instead it issues an Income and Expenditure account which is virtually the same thing. The word 'surplus' is substituted for the word profit if there has been more income than expenditure, ie Surplus of Income over Expenditure. If there is a loss this is referred to an Excess of Expenditure over Income.

THE BALANCE SHEET

Sarah's accountants are able to produce her balance sheet quite easily from her trial balance. They will do this in four stages:

Stage 1
The accountants will extract all the balances in the Ledgers and the Cash Book to produce the trial balance.

```
            Trial Balance as at 31 May 19__
                                    DR        CR
                                    £         £
        Purchases                 36000
        Sales                               48500
        Equipment                  8000
        Debtors                    2000
        Creditors                            3500
        Expenses                   3500
        Cash at Bank               7500
        Capital                              5000

                                  57000     57000
```

Stage 2
They will then ask Sarah for the value of her closing stock at cost price. Sarah tells them this is £3000.

The accountants then prepare her Trading and Profit and Loss account.

```
Trading and Profit and Loss Account for the year ended 31 May 19__

                         £                                £
   Purchases           36000      Sales                 48500
   Gross Profit c/d    15500      Closing stock          3000

                       51500                             51500

   Expenses             3500      Gross Profit b/d      15500
   Net Profit          12000

                       15500                             15500
```

Stage 3
The accountants will now rewrite the trial balance, this time leaving out the entries they used in the Trading and Profit and Loss account – namely purchases, sales and expenses.

They will then *add* in the stock figure as a debit (because it is an asset).

TEST YOURSELF

Can you prepare the new trial balance, after the Trading and Profit and Loss accounts have been completed? Follow the instructions given above to list the items required but *don't* try to balance it. You will find the answer just before the next Review Quiz.

CHECK IT YOURSELF

There is one missing, mystery figure needed to make this balance. To help you work out what it is the balance has been filled in for you.

If you are really stuck look back to the Trading and Profit and Loss accounts on the last page for a clue!

Stage 4

After this has been completed all that needs doing is for the new trial balance to be 'converted' to balance sheet style. The entries are identical – only the layout is different.

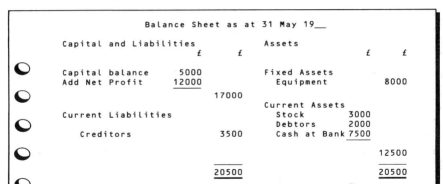

```
                    Balance Sheet as at 31 May 19__

        Capital and Liabilities              Assets
                              £      £                        £      £
   ○
        Capital balance      5000       Fixed Assets
        Add Net Profit      12000          Equipment              8000
   ○
                                  17000
                                            Current Assets
        Current Liabilities                    Stock       3000
                                               Debtors      2000
   ○       Creditors               3500        Cash at Bank 7500
   ○
                                                                 12500
   ○
                                  20500                          20500
```

SPECIAL NOTE

Hopefully you remembered the layout yourself from the first part of this chapter. You may also have remembered that net profit is added to the capital in a balance sheet because this was also mentioned. We have therefore come full circle – from balance sheets to double-entry to trial balances and Profit and Loss accounts and back to balance sheets again.

Some of you may have noticed that the balance sheet is set out in a different way from other accounts – credits are listed on the left and debits on the right. This doesn't matter as a balance sheet is *not* a part of the double-entry system. In fact, there is no logical reason why it should be the wrong way round – except tradition!

Balancing the capital and drawings accounts

In reality, rather than show the net profit separately on the new Trial Balance (as above) Sarah's Accountants would have

- added the net profit to the original capital figure brought forward at the beginning of the year
- subtracted any drawings for the year
- balanced and closed the capital account and the drawings account
- added the *final* new capital balance into the Trial Balance.

Let us assume that on 3 Feb Sarah had withdrawn £2000 from the bank for drawings. Her balanced Capital and Drawings Accounts are shown below.

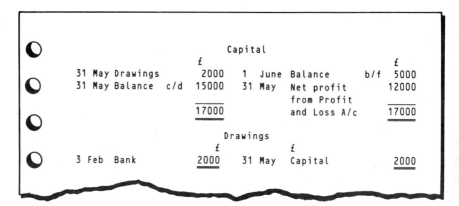

```
                              Capital
                           £                                    £
31 May  Drawings          2000   1  June  Balance      b/f    5000
31 May  Balance    c/d   15000   31 May   Net profit          12000
                                          from Profit
                         17000            and Loss A/c         17000

                              Drawings
                           £                                    £
 3 Feb   Bank             2000   31 May   Capital              2000
```

Her Balance Sheet will now look like this:

```
                  Balance Sheet as at 31 May 199_
      Capital and Liabilities          Assets
                         £      £                      £      £
      Capital Balance   5000           Fixed Assets
      Add Net Profit   12000           Equipment            8000
                       17000
      Less Drawings     2000           Current Assets
                              15000
                                       Stock          3000
      Current Liabilities              Debtors        2000
                                       Cash at Bank   5500
      Creditors                3500                         10500
                              18500                         18500
```

TEST YOURSELF

From the figures given below, can you prepare the final accounts for Roberta Knowles as at 31 August 19–. Start with her trial balance and work through until you have produced her balance sheet.

Purchases £40000   Sales £52000   Equipment £6500
Debtors £3000   Creditors £4000   Expenses £4500
Cash at Bank £6000   Capital £4000

Note that her closing stock on 31 August was £2000.

Check all your final documents with your tutor.

SECTION REVIEW

Having completed this section, you should now be able to:

1   Prepare a trial balance.

2   Explain the errors which would be highlighted by creating a trial balance and those which would not.

3   Calculate gross and net profit using double entry accounts.

4   Compile a Trading and Profit and Loss Account.

5   Extract a Trial Balance after completion of a Trading and Profit and Loss Account and convert this to balance sheet format.

Here is the answer to the Text Yourself on page 185.

```
                    Trial Balance as at 31 May 19__
          (After Trading and Profit and Loss Accounts completed)

                                        DR          CR
                                        £           £
          Equipment                     8000
          Debtors                       2000
          Creditors                                 3500
          Cash at Bank                  7500
          Stock                         3000
          Capital                                   5000
          ???                                       ???
                                       _____      _____
                                        20500       20500
```

True or False?

1 A trial balance will show up faulty addition in the accounts.

2 The Returns Inwards account results in a debit balance.

3 The major aim of most businesses is to make a profit.

4 Income Tax is paid on gross profit whereas Corporation Tax is paid on net profit.

5 Stock is a debit item because it is an asset.

Complete the blanks . . .

6 Limited companies have to have their accounts .... every year.

7 Credit balances = ...

8 Sales minus (......................................) = gross profit.

Work it out

9 **a** A business shows the following balances as at 31 March 199–. Draw up a Trial Balance with the items in their correct order:

Debtors £6800   Sales £48 500   Drawings £5000
Capital £20 000   Cash £200   General expenses £1000
Rent £2000   Purchases £39 000   Advertising £1500
Equipment £5000   Bank £17 100   Creditors £9100

9 **b** You are informed that the unsold stock for the year is valued at £3 000. Using this information:

i Use double entry accounts to calculate the gross profit for the year.

ii Continue using double entry accounts to calculate the net profit figure (ie draw up a Trading and Profit and Loss Account.)

iii Make out the Trial Balance after the Trading and Profit and Loss Accounts are completed and then convert this to Balance Sheet format.

Section 5 – VAT Returns and VAT Accounts

The one item we have so far ignored in relation to Sarah's accounts is **VAT – Value Added Tax**. It may be that if Sarah's business is only small she does not need to be registered for VAT but as her business grows and her turnover increases she will have to keep a careful watch to make sure she does not go over the limit without informing the VAT office.

CHECK IT YOURSELF

Can you remember what turnover is? It is the value of the goods *sold* over a given period.

What is Value Added Tax?

VAT is a tax which is *added on* to goods every time they change hands, eg:

- from timber merchant to furniture manufacturer
- from manufacturer to wholesaler
- from wholesaler to retailer
- from retailer to customer.

The current VAT rate is 15%. This can be changed by the government and has been altered in previous budgets.

How it works

If the timber merchant sold wood to the furniture manufacturer for £200 he would have to add on VAT of £30 (ie 15% of £200).

The wood would therefore cost the manufacturer £230. When he makes it into furniture he may sell it to the wholesaler for £500 + VAT, making a total of £575.

The wholesaler sells the furniture to the retailer for £700 + VAT, making £805.

Finally, the retailer sells it to the customer for £1200 + VAT, a sum of £1380.

But

Businesses do not pay all the tax every time. They only need to pay the *difference* between the tax they collect (called **output tax**) and tax they pay out (called **input tax**).

The furniture manufacturer in our example has collected £75 VAT from the wholesaler, but he paid out £30 to the timber merchant. He therefore only needs to pay £45 to Her Majesty's Customs and Excise Office (the government department which collects VAT).

VAT terms

There are four main VAT terms you need to know.
These are easy to remember if you think of them as follows:

Goods in (purchases) = ***in*puts**

Tax paid on goods in = ***in*put tax**

Goods out (sales) = ***out*puts**

Tax collected on goods out = ***out*put tax**

TEST YOURSELF

In the above example, how much would

- the wholesaler   and
- the retailer

have to pay HM Customs and Excise Office in VAT?

CHECK IT YOURSELF

- Look up your local VAT office in the telephone directory.
- Find out the current level of turnover a business is allowed to have:
  a) per quarter   and
  b) per year
  before they must be registered for VAT.
- As a group, collect information on VAT. Useful booklets include:
  - *Should I be Registered for VAT?*
  - *The Ins and Outs of VAT*
  - *Filling in your VAT Return*
  - *VAT Guidelines* (current edition)

  The last book is absolutely essential as it contains all the current information and regulations on VAT. It will be referred to again later in this chapter.

Zero-rated goods

Not all goods are liable for VAT and organisations which deal only in zero-rated goods are normally not required to register, even if their turnover exceeds the limit.

Examples of zero-rated goods are food (but not meals in restaurants and take-aways), books and newspapers, children's clothes and shoes, prescriptions and exported goods.

In addition, some services are exempt from VAT, including insurance, education and medical services provided by doctors and dentists.

Registering for VAT

Businesses which deal in taxable goods and who are nearing the level of turnover allowed have to contact their local Customs and Excise Office and obtain a registration form.

Once this has been processed they are allocated a VAT Registration Number which must be quoted on all their invoices and credit notes. Usually every quarter the VAT Central Unit sends the organisation a VAT Return which must be completed and returned within *one* month of the end of the period covered by that Return. Therefore a Return for the period 1 January – 31 March must be received by the VAT Central Unit no later than 30 April. Organisations which send in late returns can be charged a penalty in addition to the VAT owing.

About 18 months after registering, a VAT Inspector will visit the premises and examine the accounts to make sure everything is in order. After this, visits will be made about every two or three years and the organisation must have all its business documents and accounts to hand.

SPECIAL NOTE

Most organisations complete their VAT Returns every quarter – as shown in the examples in this chapter. However, it is possible to arrange to complete them monthly – or even annually. You can check the details in *VAT Guidelines*.

VAT and accounts

Organisations which register for VAT *must* keep separate records of VAT collected and paid. This means that the books of account must be adapted for VAT.

- The Day Books are extended so that additional columns are used to record the amount before VAT, the VAT amount and the total including VAT.
- A VAT account is opened in the General Ledger in which all VAT amounts are recorded. The balance in this account at the end of each quarter is therefore the amount due to (or from) the VAT Central Unit.

Therefore if Sarah registered for VAT, her transactions would be recorded slightly differently than before.

How it works

Sarah *buys* goods in February as follows:

3 February	£500 + VAT	Allwrite Ltd
10 February	£800 + VAT	Business Machines Ltd
23 February	£2 300 + VAT	Allwrite Ltd

We will also assume that she returns some faulty goods:

| 24 February | £100 + VAT | Business Machines Ltd |

She will record these transactions as follows:

Purchases Day Book

Date	Supplier	Invoice No	Total excl VAT	VAT	Total inc VAT
3 Feb	Allwrite Ltd	KL/3017	£ 500	£ 75	£ 575
10 Feb	Business Machines Ltd	PP920	£ 800	£120	£ 920
23 Feb	Allwrite Ltd	KL/3112	£2 300	£345	£2 645
			£3 600	£540	£4 140

Returns Outwards Day Book

Date	Supplier	Credit Note No	Total excl VAT	VAT	Total inc VAT
24 Feb	Business Machines Ltd	PL540	£100	£15	£115
			£100	£15	£115

Purchases Ledger
Allwrite Ltd

DR				CR
	£			£
		3 Feb	Purchases	575
		23 Feb	Purchases	2 645

Business Machines Ltd

DR		£	CR		£
24 Feb	Returns Outwards	115	10 Feb	Purchases	920

General Ledger
Purchases

DR		£	CR		£
28 Feb	Credit purchases for the month	3600			

Returns Outwards

DR		£	CR		£
			28 Feb	Returns for the month	100

Value Added Tax

DR		£	CR		£
28 Feb	VAT on Purchases	540	28 Feb	VAT on Returns Outwards	15

SPECIAL NOTE

Note carefully exactly which amounts have been transferred to each account.

- The Purchases Ledger Accounts show the *total including VAT*.
- The General Ledger Accounts for Purchases and Returns Outwards show the *total excluding VAT*.
- The General Ledger VAT Account shows *only VAT*.
- The Day Books show *all* amounts.

TEST YOURSELF

Exactly the same procedure is used to record Sales. Draw up the Sales Day Book, Returns Inwards Day Book, Sales Ledger and General Ledger Accounts for Sales, Returns Inwards and VAT and record the following transactions. Remember that VAT on Sales is entered in the *credit* column of the VAT account and the VAT on Returns Inwards in the *debit* column.

Sarah *sold* goods in February as follows:

5 February	£ 900 + VAT	B Noble	Invoice SB/4875
14 February	£1200 + VAT	D Webster	Invoice SB/4876
27 February	£1900 + VAT	B Noble	Invoice SB/4877

Goods returned to her during that month were:

| 18 February | £200 + VAT | B Noble | Credit Note RT/42 |

Check your completed accounts with your tutor.

The VAT account

Because the VAT account shows all the VAT amounts it can be balanced at the end of the quarter to show how much is:

- owing to HM Customs and Excise (a *credit* balance)
- due from HM Customs and Excise (a *debit* balance)

When payment is made this is recorded on the payments side of the Cash Book (CR) and in the VAT Account (DR). A payment received would obviously be recorded on the receipts side of the Cash Book (DR) and in the VAT Account (CR).

Because the VAT account now shows a zero balance it can therefore be used to record VAT transactions for the next quarter.

The following example shows Sarah's VAT Account at the end of the VAT period. We have assumed that she purchased and sold goods in the following two months but neither received nor sent back any returns.

General Ledger
Value Added Tax

DR					CR
		£			£
28 Feb	VAT on Purchases	540	28 Feb	VAT on Sales	600
28 Feb	VAT on Returns Inwards	30	28 Feb	VAT on Returns Outwards	15
31 Mar	VAT on Purchases	720	31 Mar	VAT on Sales	950
30 Apr	VAT on Purchases	640	30 Apr	VAT on Sales	880
30 Apr	Balance c/d	515			
		2445			2445
21 May	Bank	515	30 Apr	Balance c/d	515

When an organisation is registered for VAT it must keep all its records for at least six years. This includes copies of related business documents such as invoices and credit notes. An organisation which loses an invoice from a supplier *must* obtain a copy – the statement does not count as a support document for VAT. It is therefore essential that great care is always taken of all invoices and credit notes.

TEST YOURSELF

In many firms the accounts are completed direct from primary documents, ie invoices sent and received and credit notes sent and received.

From the work you have done so far, can you identify *which* accounts books, and which accounts within each, would be used to record:

1   An invoice received for £200 + VAT from Business Machines Ltd
2   An invoice sent out for £560 + VAT to D Webster
3   A credit note received for £23 + VAT from Allwrite Ltd
4   A credit note sent out for £10 + VAT to B Noble.

CHECK IT YOURSELF

Your organisation is about to register for VAT and your boss has asked you to find out the following information. Using *VAT Guidelines* and other leaflets can you find the rights answers for her?

- Are accounts kept on computer disc or microfilm acceptable to VAT Inspectors?
- If the organisation forgets to charge VAT on an invoice (by mistake) would it still have to pay the amount it should have charged to the VAT Central Unit?
- What happens if someone loses the VAT Return? Can we take a photocopy to be on the safe side and send this in if the original goes missing?

COMPLETING A VAT RETURN

A VAT Return is already preprinted with various items of information:

- the name and address of the business and the person in that business registered with the VAT Central Unit
- the period dates which that Return covers

- the VAT Registration Number of that business
- the date by which the Return must reach the VAT Central Unit
  See the illustration on page 200.

To complete the VAT Return, the accounts staff must extract and calculate the following figures from the accounts in the General Ledger:

From the VAT Account
- VAT paid on purchases that quarter less VAT paid on any Returns Outwards (purchases returned.) This is the Input Tax.
- VAT collected on sales that quarter less VAT collected on any Returns Inwards (sales returned.) This is the Output Tax.

From the Purchases Account
- The total value of all purchases *excluding* VAT for the quarter.

From the Returns Outwards Account
- The total value of all Returns Outwards *excluding* VAT for the quarter.

From the Sales Account
- The total value of all sales *excluding* VAT for the quarter.

From the Returns Inwards Account
- The total value of all Returns Inwards *excluding* VAT for the quarter.

 TEST YOURSELF

From Sarah's VAT account shown on page 194 can you calculate her Output Tax and her Input Tax?

If you *subtract* her output tax from her input tax you should reach the same figure as the balance shown in her VAT account. This is Sarah's **tax due** for the quarter.

 Calculating Outputs and Inputs

The figures extracted *excluding* VAT are used to calculate Sarah's Inputs less VAT and Outputs less VAT. This is done as follows:

- *subtract* the total value of Returns Outwards from the total value of all purchases to calculate Inputs less VAT. Round your figure to the nearest whole pound.
- *subtract* the total value of Returns Inwards from the total value of all sales to calculate Outputs less VAT. Again round your figure to the nearest whole pound.

TEST YOURSELF

Sarah's full accounts for the quarter show that, *excluding* VAT:
- her total purchases = £12666.65
- her total sales = £16199.98
- her returns outwards = £100
- her returns inwards = £200

From these figures can you calculate:

- her Inputs less VAT
- her Outputs less VAT.

Remember to round these to the nearest whole pound. If you do this correctly you will find that her Input Tax figure is (within a few pence) 15% of her Inputs less VAT.

EXPENSES

Sarah has not only paid VAT on her purchases, she has also paid VAT on other expenditure essential to run her business – stationery, equipment, petrol, her telephone account etc.

Once she is registered herself she can reclaim the VAT on these expenses. She can only do this if:

- the expense is allowable for VAT
- she has an invoice from a VAT registered supplier to back up her claim.

Therefore, in her accounts, her expenses will now be recorded *excluding* VAT and she will enter the amount of VAT paid on these in the *debit* column of her VAT account. In this way she is adding the VAT to her inputs and her Input Tax figure will increase. Because tax due is Output Tax less Input Tax her tax due will now be reduced by the VAT she has paid on her expenses.

SPECIAL NOTE

If you find expenses confusing, simply think of them as another type of purchase (input). Therefore:

Purchases of goods plus allowable expenses = Inputs
Tax paid on purchases and allowable expenses = Input Tax

CHECK IT YOURSELF

Using the *VAT Guidelines* find out:

- if Sarah can reclaim VAT paid on a hotel accommodation bill whilst she was in London on a business trip
- whether Sarah has to include in her outputs VAT on drinks purchased by staff in the vending machine near the canteen.

SPECIAL NOTE

The regulations on VAT are many and there are severe penalties for organisations who claim VAT back on non-allowable expenses (such as a business dinner in a restaurant). *Never* guess what is or is not allowable, you must check with a supervisor or the local VAT office.

CHECK IT YOURSELF

1 Work out how much Sarah can add to her input tax if:
- she has paid allowable expense bills of £750 plus VAT
- she has also paid petrol bills (where VAT is inclusive) of £184.00. (You should be familiar with this from previous chapters.)

   What is her new input tax figure?

2 Rewrite her VAT Account to include the VAT you have just calculated for Sarah's expenses. Compare your new balance with the original balance. You should find that the balance has been reduced by the additional amount of VAT you added to the debit column.

   What is her new tax due figure?

SPECIAL NOTE

In reality, of course, her expenses and the VAT on these would be entered in the accounts as they occurred. For simplicity, we will treat the VAT on expenses as one entry, which you can write in under the last day of the quarter, ie 30 April.

Expenses and Inputs less VAT

If Sarah claims VAT back on allowable expenses then she must also add the total of her expenses excluding VAT (as shown in her expense accounts) to the total value of her inputs excluding VAT to calculate her Inputs less VAT figure.

TEST YOURSELF

1   Calculate the figure for Sarah's expenses, excluding VAT, from the information given above.
2   Add this figure to the figure for Inputs less VAT you calculated previously to obtain her revised amount for Inputs less VAT.

If you do this correctly you should find that your new Input Tax figure is still about 15% of your Inputs less VAT.

VAT formula

Sarah used the following formula to calculate the VAT:

Output Tax – Input Tax

Because her Output Tax is greater than her Input Tax she owes the difference to HM Customs and Excise. This is also confirmed by the fact that her VAT account shows a *credit* balance.

If her Input Tax had been greater than her Output Tax, then Sarah can reclaim the difference from HM Customs and Excise. This would also be confirmed by her VAT account which would show a *debit* balance.

SPECIAL NOTE

Input Tax may be greater than Output Tax when, for instance, a company exports most of its goods. VAT is chargeable on imports (ie it must be paid in the usual way) but exports are *exempt* from VAT. Therefore if tax is paid on purchases and then all the goods are exported, a considerable amount of VAT has been paid out but none collected. The amount paid out (Input Tax) can therefore be claimed back.

An organisation must, however, support this claim with evidence of exports made.

PAYING VAT

When Sarah has calculated her figures and the VAT she owes she must:

- complete her VAT Return and make sure this is signed and dated.
- pay HM Customs and Excise. She can do this either:
  - by cheque, making it payable to HM Customs and Excise and writing her VAT Registration Number on the reverse
  - by credit transfer. To do this she must ask the local VAT office for a supply of credit transfer forms *in advance*.

CHECK IT YOURSELF

Sarah's completed VAT Return for the figures you have been calculating is shown below. Check that the figures entered agree with those you calculated and note how her entries have been made.

Value Added Tax Return
For the period
1 February 199- to 30 April 199-

For Official Use

HM Customs and Excise

Registration Number	Period
521 4765 89	1

Ms Sarah Barnes
Quasar Office Supplies
14 Cathedral Close
LINTON BRIDGE
N Yorkshire

You could be liable to a financial penalty if your completed return and all the VAT payable are not received by the due date.

Due date: 31 May 199-

For Official Use

Before you fill in this form please read the notes on the back. Complete all boxes clearly in ink, writing 'none' where necessary. Don't put a dash or leave any box blank. If there are no pence write "00" in the pence column. Do not enter more than one amount in any box.

		£	p
VAT due in this period on **sales** and other outputs	1	2400	00
VAT reclaimed in this period on **purchases** and other inputs	2	2021	50
Net VAT to be paid to Customs or reclaimed by you (**Difference between boxes 1 and 2**)	3	378	50
Value of **outputs** (pounds only) excluding any VAT	4	16 000	00
Value of **inputs** (pounds only) excluding any VAT	5	13 477	00

Retail schemes. If you have used any of the schemes in the period covered by this return please enter the appropriate letter(s) in this box.

If you are enclosing a payment please tick (✓) this box. ✓

DECLARATION by the signatory to be completed by or on behalf of the person named above.
I, ...SARAH BARNES........ declare that the
(Full name of signatory in BLOCK LETTERS)
information given above is true and complete.
Signature ....Sarah Barnes........ Date ...20 MAY... 19 9-

VAT 100 CD 1911/N7(12/89)   F 3790(

SPECIAL NOTE

Errors on the VAT Return should be clearly crossed through and the correct figure inserted. Errors not noticed until *after* the form has been submitted are more serious. The local VAT office must be contacted *immediately* the mistake is noticed as organisations can be liable for interest on any amounts underpaid in a quarter.

Technology update

Many organisations today use computerised accounts packages to do all their double-entry booking, VAT returns and to produce their trial balance, Trading and Profit and Loss account and balance sheet automatically at the end of the year.

Using such a package means that up-to-date information on the financial situation of the company can be accessed at any time at the touch of a key.

SECTION REVIEW

Having completed this section, you should now be able to:

1   Explain how the VAT system operates.

2   Differentiate between output tax and input tax.

3   Explain the difference between zero-rated goods and exemptions from VAT and give examples of each.

4   Describe the procedure for registering for VAT.

5   Look up general VAT queries in VAT Guide books and leaflets.

6   Write up accounts from business documents involving VAT calculations.

7   Draw up a VAT Account.

8   Calculate VAT due from ledgers.

9   Calculate VAT inclusive amounts.

10   Calculate outputs less VAT and inputs less VAT.

11   Complete a VAT Return.

12   State the procedures available for paying VAT.

True or False?

1 VAT is paid every twelve months.

2 A penalty can be levied on companies which send in a late return.

3 VAT paid on all expenses is reclaimable.

4 VAT can be paid by credit transfer.

5 The amount of VAT paid on purchases is called Input Tax.

Complete the blanks ...

6 Cheques for VAT should be made payable to ....

7 On the reverse of the cheque should be written the ....
....

8 VAT records must be kept for a least .... years.

Work it out

9 For the next quarter, Sarah's General Ledger shows the following VAT exclusive figures:

Sales Account	–	May =	£5200
		June =	£4050
		July =	£5000
Purchases Account	–	May =	£2000
		June =	£3500
		July =	£3300
Returns Inwards Account	–	May =	£210
		June =	NIL
		July =	£610
Returns Outwards Account	–	May =	£200
		June =	£120
		July =	£320
Expense Accounts	–	Total for quarter = £782.61	

Note that the total amount of VAT reclaimable on expenses is £117.39, allowing for the fact that some expenses were plus VAT and others were VAT inclusive.

From the above figures can you:

a Calculate her VAT on Sales, Returns Inwards, Purchases and Returns Outwards for the quarter.

b Draw up and balance her VAT account to incorporate the VAT amounts and also the VAT reclaimable on expenses.

c Calculate:

- her Input Tax
- her Output Tax
- her Inputs less VAT
- her Outputs less VAT
- her VAT due.

Note that if you do this correctly the amount owing will be the same as your credit balance in the VAT account.

10 From all the work you have done in this chapter, can you list the main financial functions and obligations of an Accounts Department for a new employee who is uncertain of the work carried out there? Check your answer with your tutor.

Appendix – Computerised Accounts Packages

There is a variety of accounts packages on the market today –
many aimed at small businesses. A good accounts package will:

- keep a record of all sales to each customer on credit
- keep a record of all cash sales
- produce invoices, credit notes and statements
- list amounts outstanding (on an aged debtors' report)
- keep a record of all purchases made (by supplier and type of
  goods)
- keep a record of all accounts paid/still to be paid to suppliers
- record all bank transactions
- undertake all the book-keeping required
- print out a variety of 'reports', eg trial balance, balance sheet,
  VAT returns, bank analysis, audit report and so on.

It can therefore save the owner a lot of work – he doesn't really
even need to know how to use a conventional book-keeping
system, though it helps if he does!

Starting up

When the package is first purchased, and before it is used, the
owner must make out a list of **headings** that he will use to record
his accounts. If he uses a manual accounting system he can use
his existing account headings. Each account will be given a
number and categorised under the following main headings:

- sales (different categories will be listed under a different
  number)
- other income
- purchases (this refers to purchases of stock)
- expenses and overheads
- capital
- liabilities (eg any money he owes, such as a bank loan)
- fixed assets (eg his shop)
- current assets
- current liabilities (eg money he owes for VAT).

When he first plans out the numbers he will use the owner must allow for additional categories to be added at a later date. The program will also tell him which numbers he *cannot* use – certain ones will be allocated, eg for total sales, total purchases etc, and these totals will automatically be calculated by the computer from the information it is given.

His remaining task is to enter his opening balances for each account, eg his money in the bank, capital etc.

Customer/supplier records
Our owner will now need to refer to the part of the package where he records details on:

- all his customers, eg name and address, telephone number, discount allowed etc
- all his suppliers, eg name and address, telephone number etc.

This is set up usually just like a database system, with record cards to complete.

There will usually be blank fields for items such as 'amount owing' or 'total amount outstanding'. These fields are automatically completed by the computer when a sale or purchase is made.

SPECIAL NOTE
On most systems the user does *not* have to allocate account numbers to his customers and suppliers – this is done automatically by the computer.

Cash and credit transactions
The computer divides all transactions into two types:

- cash transactions – where payment is instant (whether it is by cash, cheque or credit card) as in a shop
- credit transactions – where a customer is given several weeks to pay and the transaction necessitates an invoice and a statement at the end of the month.

Entering cash transactions
This is usually quite simple. Under the cash part of the package

the owner lists (usually daily) all the money he has received for *each* type of goods he sells. Most tills can analyse sales by type of goods so he could use his till audit roll for this information.

Against each amount received he therefore inserts the account number for that particular sale. The computer then does two things:

- it records his takings as a *debit* entry to cash on premises and
- makes a *credit* entry under the sales account he specified.

It has therefore carried out double entry!

If, the following day, he informs the computer he has banked the money he tells it the number for his bank account so that the computer can

- *debit* his bank account and *credit* his cash on premises account.

 Entering credit transactions

This is carried out by calling up the customer record card and listing the items sold. The computer will then print out an invoice for the goods and *automatically* deduct any discount stated on the record.

At the same time it *debits* the customer's account and *credits* the *sales* account. At the end of the month the owner can instruct the computer to issue statements for all customers with outstanding accounts.

When the money is received he calls up the customer's record again, notes down details of the payment and the computer marks the appropriate invoices as paid, *credits* the customer's account and *debits* the bank account.

 Buying goods

When he buys goods the process is the same, depending on whether he buys for cash or on credit. For credit transactions he would call up his supplier's record card and record the purchase.

The computer would then *debit* the appropriate purchases account and *credit* the supplier's account. When he pays his bill the supplier's account would then be *debited* and his bank account (or cash account) *credited* accordingly.

Most accounts packages will automatically print out a remittance advice to accompany the cheque when the account is paid.

Mistakes

You must remember that, at all times, the computer has to be informed of the *numbers* of the accounts involved in any transaction. It is, of course, possible to make a mistake and enter the wrong account number or amount by accident. If this happens, packages vary in their ability to sort out the problem. With most of them it is necessary to make the adjustment by making opposite entries, rather than just cancelling out the wrong ones.

Because correcting mistakes can be complicated – and uncorrected mistakes disastrous – it is important that you:

- *think* what you are doing!
- take extreme care not to transpose figures
- carry out a rationality check when you see the answer – does it *look right* in relation to the figures you have been dealing with? If not – investigate!

Month end

At the end of each month the computer will probably prompt the user to run the month end reports. This will print out a copy of all the account 'books' for the month which should be stored safely.

The month end function then usually tidies all the files by removing all the paid items, and automatically increases the accounting month number by one.

Lists and reports

A variety of lists and reports can be produced, at any time, at the touch of a key. These can include:

- customer list with names and addresses
- aged debtors or aged creditors analysis

- sales and purchase daybooks
- audit list (showing every transaction that month)
- money received (or paid)
- list of suppliers.

In addition the employer can produce:

- trading and profit and loss account
- trial balance
- balance sheet
- VAT return.

Integrated accounts package

The more sophisticated an accounts package the more difficult it can be to use, unless you work with it every day. Some of the more advanced ones are automatically integrated with a wages (payroll) package so that wages totals are automatically transferred to the wages account and debited and the firm's bank account credited with the total amount paid out.